STUDENT RIGHTS IN A
NEW AGE OF ACTIVISM

By Anna Collins

Portions of this book originally appeared in *Students' Rights* by Kate Burns.

LUCENT
P R E S S

Published in 2020 by
Lucent Press, an Imprint of Greenhaven Publishing, LLC
353 3rd Avenue
Suite 255
New York, NY 10010

Designer: Andrea Davison-Bartolotta
Editor: Jennifer Lombardo

Cataloging-in-Publication Data

Names: Collins, Anna.
Title: Student rights in a new age of activism / Anna Collins.
Description: New York : Lucent Press, 2020. | Series: Hot topics | Includes index.
Identifiers: ISBN 9781534568167 (pbk.) | ISBN 9781534568174 (library bound) | ISBN
9781534568181 (ebook)
Subjects: LCSH: Students–Legal status, laws, etc.–United States–Juvenile literature. | Students-
-Civil rights–United States–Juvenile literature. | Educational law and legislation–United
States–Juvenile literature. | Student movements–Juvenile literature.
Classification: LCC KF4150.C65 2020 | DDC 344.73'0793–dc23

Printed in China

Some of the images in this book illustrate individuals who are models. The depictions do
not imply actual situations or events

CPSIA compliance information: Batch #BW20KL: For further information contact Greenhaven Publishing LLC, New York,
New York at 1-844-317-7404.

Please visit our website, www.greenhavenpublishing.com. For a free color catalog of all our
high-quality books, call toll free 1-844-317-7404 or fax 1-844-317-7405.

CONTENTS

FOREWORD   4

INTRODUCTION   6
The Evolution of Education

CHAPTER 1   10
The Right to a Free and Equal Education

CHAPTER 2   28
Freedom of Expression

CHAPTER 3   44
Freedom of the School Press

CHAPTER 4   58
Freedom of Religion

CHAPTER 5   74
Privacy Rights

NOTES   88

DISCUSSION QUESTIONS   94

ORGANIZATIONS TO CONTACT   96

FOR MORE INFORMATION   98

INDEX   100

PICTURE CREDITS   103

ABOUT THE AUTHOR   104

Adolescence is a time when many people begin to take notice of the world around them. News channels, blogs, and talk radio shows are constantly promoting one view or another; very few are unbiased. Young people also hear conflicting information from parents, friends, teachers, and acquaintances. Often, they will hear only one side of an issue or be given flawed information. People who are trying to support a particular viewpoint may cite inaccurate facts and statistics on their blogs, and news programs present many conflicting views of important issues in our society. In a world where it seems everyone has a platform to share their thoughts, it can be difficult to find unbiased, accurate information about important issues.

It is not only facts that are important. In blog posts, in comments on online videos, and on talk shows, people will share opinions that are not necessarily true or false, but can still have a strong impact. For example, many young people struggle with their body image. Seeing or hearing negative comments about particular body types online can have a huge effect on the way someone views himself or herself and may lead to depression and anxiety. Although it is important not to keep information hidden from young people under the guise of protecting them, it is equally important to offer encouragement on issues that affect their mental health.

The titles in the Hot Topics series provide readers with different viewpoints on important issues in today's society. Many of these issues, such as students' rights, are of immediate concern to young people. This series aims to give readers factual context on these crucial topics in a way that lets them form their own opinions. The facts presented throughout also serve to empower readers to help themselves or support people they know who are struggling with many of the challenges adolescents face today. Although negative viewpoints are not ignored or downplayed, this series allows young people to see that the challenges they face are not insurmountable. As increasing numbers of young adults join public debates, especially regarding their own rights, learning the facts as well as the views of others will help them decide where they stand—and understand what they are fighting for.

Quotes encompassing all viewpoints are presented and cited so readers can trace them back to their original source, verifying for themselves whether the information comes from a reputable place. Additional books and websites are listed, giving readers a starting point from which to continue their own research. Chapter questions encourage discussion, allowing young people to hear and understand their classmates' points of view as they further solidify their own. Full-color photographs and enlightening charts provide a deeper understanding of the topics at hand. All of these features augment the informative text, helping young people understand the world they live in and formulate their own opinions concerning the best way they can improve it.

The Evolution of Education

In the United States, the rights of people under the age of 18 are a hotly debated and frequently misunderstood topic. Some adults believe that since students have to abide by the rules their schools and parents set, they have no right to challenge any of those rules. Students themselves may also feel that they do not have any rights, especially when schools overreach their boundaries and try to suppress their students' rights. In reality, certain rights are protected for students by the U.S. Constitution. What exactly are these rights, and what can students do when they are violated?

Access to Education

Historically, the first debate about student rights arose over the question of whether everyone was entitled to a public education. As understood today, public education means schooling provided by the government and paid for by taxes; however, public education in America arose out of an early union between the church and the state. The Puritans of the Massachusetts Bay Colony during the 17th century started the first state-sponsored schools, whose curriculum combined religious and academic instruction for all boys and occasionally for girls. The oldest continuously operating public school in the United States is the Boston Latin School, which was founded in 1635. Outside of Puritan Massachusetts, though, religious diversity and class division made public education more challenging. Male children of wealthy landowners were the only ones who consistently received an education; if schools did not exist—which was the

The Boston Latin School (shown here) is considered one of the best schools in Massachusetts. In the past, it was only open to white male students, but today, girls account for 54 percent of the student body, and people of color account for 53 percent.

case in many colonies at that time, especially in the South—these male children were tutored at home. Girls and women, poor children, indentured servants, and slaves often went without any formal schooling. When girls did receive an education, the emphasis was placed on what they needed to know to be good wives and mothers; for example, they were often taught how to read but not how to write. In contrast, boys were taught subjects that would help them find a good career later in life.

It was not until the Revolutionary period that a pioneering education agenda began to take shape. At this time, a new enthusiasm for civic duty to one's community outweighed the traditional emphasis on religious training that dominated schools for so many years. Influenced by the writing and ratification of the U.S. Constitution, American education began to take shape as a way to achieve national unity. It was at this time that common schools, which educated students of all ages in one room with one teacher, began to emerge. According to the American Board for the Certification of Teacher Excellence, "Students did not attend these schools for free. Parents paid tuition, provided housing for the school teacher, or contributed other commodities in exchange for their children being allowed to attend the school."[1] Since money was not the only way for parents to pay for their children's education, even poor students could attend school, although they may not have done so consistently if they were needed at home.

One-room schoolhouses still exist in more rural parts of the country, but they have decreased from 190,000 in 1919 to fewer than 400 a century later.

At the turn of the 19th century, a humanitarian movement to provide free education to the children of the poor—including free schools for black children—was thriving in the North. It was argued that children needed basic reading skills to work in the manufacturing trades, and that strong values and a love of learning helped to deter children from lives of crime. American philosopher and psychologist John Dewey promoted the idea that education should focus on helping children reach their full potential to become active members of society—a concept that spread throughout the country between 1890 and 1930. More than ever before, school was seen as the melting pot that could level economic differences, blend racial differences, and teach children what it meant to be American. As a result of that thinking, 19th-century court cases and legislation in the United States laid the foundation for the public support of schools from elementary to college levels. After the American Civil War, this movement spread to the South as well. By 1918, it was mandatory for all American children to attend school, although it was still difficult for many poorer students to attend past elementary school; many had to find jobs instead of going to high school so they could help support their families.

Cultural Changes

The circumstances of American childhood changed dramatically between 1945 and 1960. The rapid increase in the post–World War II population, called the baby boom, and postwar economic prosperity meant that more young people than ever before were free to attend school and associate with each other. Retailers and the entertainment industry recognized teens as a new market that had the freedom to spend money on clothes, amusement, popular culture, and the media. A youth movement began to develop in the 1960s and 1970s as baby boomer students demanded a space in American life for the expression of youth culture.

Along with this development, young people recognized their limited power and status in American society and began demanding more independence and power to make their own decisions. Student activism led to increased pressure for an expansion of student rights. Beginning in the 1960s, these issues came into the foreground of American society with court cases and legislation that further defined students' civil rights and civil liberties—and their appropriate limitations.

In the new millennium, those liberties and limitations continue to evolve alongside new advances in technology that complicate classic student rights issues. In particular, the issues of access to information, freedom of expression, and privacy must be revisited in relation to students using the internet and other electronic technology in school. Also, a new wave of student activism, especially directed at ending gun violence, has caused many people—both adults and students alike—to take a closer look at the rights young people have in the United States. It is likely that ever-developing innovations and social changes influencing education will ensure that student rights remain a hot topic in American society for years to come.

CHAPTER 1

The Right to a Free and Equal Education

One of the most basic rights students have is, quite simply, the right to be a student. Although education is mandatory for people until they reach the age of 16, all Americans have the right to a free and equal education until they graduate from high school or turn 21—whichever comes first. "Free" in this context means no one can be denied enrollment in a public school even if they do not have a lot of money, and "equal" means that no matter which school someone attends, they will receive the same quality of education they would at any other American public school. This applies to people of any race and gender.

These rights seem straightforward, but in practice, they are not always carried out faithfully. In the past, some people have disagreed over who these rights applied to, and in the present, some barriers exist that prevent certain students from accessing this most basic right.

Ruling Against Segregated Education

Educational conflicts played a major role in the civil rights movement of the 1950s and 1960s. By the mid-20th century, many Americans agreed that all citizens, regardless of race, gender, or class, deserved the right to an education. However, laws or customs in most parts of the country still made sure that black children attended schools that were segregated from those for white children. Equality in education could be achieved, it was argued by many white Americans, without allowing black people into all-white schools. An 1896 Supreme Court decision had declared that "separate but equal" facilities were allowed;

this meant that segregation was acceptable as long as the facilities for each race were of equal quality.

Under segregation, black-only schools were supposed to be equal to white-only schools. However, this was generally not the case.

In practice, however, the facilities for black Americans were almost always inferior, and this was no different when it came to their schools. For example, it was not uncommon in the deep southern states for black-only schools to be nothing more than small, falling-down buildings. Former Secretary of Education Rod Paige described his experience with segregation during his school years in Mississippi:

The fact that [white students] had a gym was a big deal. They played basketball on the inside. They had a big gym with lights and stuff on the inside. We played basketball on the outside with a clay court. We played up until the time that you couldn't see the hoop any more … I wanted to take band, but there was no music.

I wanted to play football, but there was no football team ... The concept of separate but equal is not at all academic for me. It is very personal. And even today ... I don't know what I missed.[2]

The civil rights movement gave voice to the many black parents and leaders who were angered by the dishonesty they saw in the "separate but equal" standard. They argued that it allowed whites to maintain their prejudices and keep the best public education resources for their own children. The controversy inspired one of the most famous civil rights court cases in American history. On behalf of the National Association for the Advancement of Colored People (NAACP), a young black lawyer named Thurgood Marshall organized the case *Brown v. Board of Education of Topeka* against several segregated school districts in the country. Marshall argued the case before the Supreme Court in December 1952; in May 1954, the Court famously ruled, in Chief Justice Earl Warren's decision, that "separate educational facilities are inherently unequal."[3] This decision overturned years of school segregation, and suddenly the term "student rights" applied to white and black students alike.

Pushback Against Forced Desegregation

Enforcing desegregation was another problem entirely. The Supreme Court justices issued no specific deadlines to integrate American schools, using a gradual approach that allowed opponents of the decision to organize massive resistance to school desegregation. By 1956, more than 100 members of Congress signed a mandate called the Southern Manifesto and promised to use any methods they could to overturn the *Brown* decision. A few scattered efforts to integrate schools in the late 1950s were met with intimidation, violence, and even bombings.

By 1964, 10 years after the *Brown* decision, only 2 percent of African American students in the South were attending formerly white-only schools. Finally recognizing the need to enforce the law, Congress passed the Civil Rights Act of 1964. Among other measures, the act authorized the federal government to withhold funding from public schools that did not integrate their

Educational Equality for Other People of Color

As immigration changed the demographic landscape of the United States between the 1970s and the 1990s, the rights of other people of color to a free and equal public education also became an issue. The rising Latinx and Asian populations in many states revealed the shortcomings of desegregation discussions that focused exclusively on black and white racial mixing. Many people of color, especially Asians, share a history of being excluded from public education. The strong suspicion and hatred of Chinese immigrants by white Americans in the 19th century was especially fierce in western territories such as California. In 1859, officials in San Francisco built a separate Chinese School, which was later renamed the Oriental Public School, and required Chinese, Japanese, and Korean children to stay away from white students. Some individual Asian Americans in smaller towns successfully resisted segregation, yet the courts did not end legal segregation in California until 1947.

In the same vein, many people assume that the plaintiffs in *Brown* were the first people of color to collectively challenge segregation in American education. However, as early as 1930, Mexican Americans were standing up to efforts in California and Texas to create separate schools for their children. For example, in Lemon Grove, California, school board officials claimed that Mexican American children, who often needed extra help becoming fluent in English, were slowing down the education of white students. The community made plans to build a school just for Mexican Americans, but their progress was interrupted when Mexican Americans in the border town filed a lawsuit against the school board for discriminating against their children. In 1931, they won their court case, *Roberto Alvarez v. the Board of Trustees of the Lemon Grove School District*, and successfully prevented segregated education more than two decades before the landmark *Brown* decision.

students. At last, the federal government could file school deseg-regation suits and pressure resisting districts to obey the law. In 1968, Marshall, serving as the first black Supreme Court justice, led the Court in requiring an immediate end to segregation.

From the late 1960s until the late 1980s, rigorous federal and local programs helped to achieve more racial integration than ever before. Many school districts began a controversial program known as busing, transporting students outside of their neighborhoods to attend schools that previously had no racial mixing. As a result, racial diversity in public schools improved even in the South, where the number of black students in previously white-only schools rose to 44 percent by 1988. Moreover, many of the predominantly black schools in southern states were provided with facilities and resources equal to those

Busing was the only way many black students could attend schools that had previously been white-only. This controversial program was largely discontinued by the 1990s.

of predominantly white schools by 1990, and more black teachers received salaries equal to those of white teachers.

Although schools are officially desegregated today, unofficial segregation persists, and some news outlets report that it has been getting worse since the 2000s. Most people in the United States attend a school that is close to where they live. Since people of color disproportionately live in poorer communities, their local public schools tend to be underfunded. White families generally tend to be wealthier, so they often live in places with better schools or have the option to send their children to better private schools further away from home. This means the schools in predominantly poor communities are generally segregated by default.

Some people do not believe this type of segregation is a problem since it is not legally enforced, but research has shown that "desegregated schools are linked to important benefits, like prejudice reduction, heightened civic engagement and analytical thinking, and better learning outcomes in general."[4] Additionally, underfunding in schools affects the quality of education the students receive. Poorer schools "have less local resources, they have fewer parents with college degrees, they have fewer two parent families where there are parents who can come spend time volunteering in the school, [and] they have a harder time attracting the best teachers."[5] They also generally have worse resources for students, such as outdated books and computers.

Some schools today have tried to overturn desegregation on their own. In 1970, Rita Jones Turner became one of the first black students to attend Vestavia Hills High School in Birmingham, Alabama, after forced desegregation. She remembered that often the school bus would not stop to pick her up; when it did and she arrived at school, she was placed into remedial classes even though she did not need extra help. At lunchtime, white students harassed her by tearing barrettes from her hair.

In 2006, Jones Turner received a note from her old school informing her of its attempt to change the policy of desegregation and force her ninth-grade son to enroll elsewhere. Specifically, the school district filed a court motion to stop forced integration. Jones Turner's own experience at Vestavia Hills remained a

VIOLATIONS OF THE RIGHT TO A FREE AND EQUAL EDUCATION

"African American, Latino, and Native American students are suspended or expelled in numbers vastly disproportionate to those of their white peers ... Students of color are more likely to drop out–or be pushed out–of school and less likely to graduate than white students ... Students of color have less access to advanced classes or programs for gifted students."

– findings from a 2000 study called *Facing the Consequences: An Examination of Racial Discrimination in U.S. Public Schools*

Rebecca Gordon, Libero Della Piana, and Terry Keleher, *Facing the Consequences: An Examination of Racial Discrimination in US Public Schools,* Race Forward, 2000, p. 2, www.raceforward.org/sites/default/files/pdf/196apdf.pdf.

painful memory, but she resented any attempts at turning back the clock on progress. "We were used, mistreated, downtrodden, and discriminated against," said Jones Turner. "I have no problem with being a sacrificial lamb for the good of the community, but to have the system back out now is not fair. They made a commitment to educate black children."[6]

The Vestavia Hills school board denied any racial motivation in wanting to halt integration; instead, the board claimed that economics forced its decision. The school said its budget could no longer handle busing black students from all the way across town. A judge ruled in favor of the school.

School segregation affects more than just schools. According to writer Roger Shuler, "The euphemism you hear in the Birmingham real-estate game is that cities such as Mountain Brook, Vestavia Hills, and Homewood have 'good schools.' That means they have overwhelmingly white schools, and many home buyers are willing to pay hugely inflated prices to live in those areas."[7] The rising cost of housing means many families of color cannot afford to live in those areas, so they cannot send their children to those schools, creating a vicious cycle of

Rights for Students with Disabilities

In the past, students with disabilities—both physical and mental—frequently had problems attending school. For example, while a school might not have officially barred a student in a wheelchair, the student might not be able to attend if the school had too many stairs and no accommodations were made to help them. Similarly, students who were blind or deaf generally had to attend separate schools, and this could present problems if there were none close by. Additionally, students with learning disabilities that caused them to get poor grades could be disciplined or expelled for not performing to acceptable standards.

In 1990, the Americans with Disabilities Act (ADA) was passed, changing life for many students. Under this law, classrooms, bathrooms, and school buses must be wheelchair accessible; students who are blind or deaf must be allowed to use devices in the classroom that make it easier for them to follow along with the lesson, and Braille textbooks must be provided for students who are blind; and disciplinary measures must take the person's disability into account. For students with learning disabilities, accommodations may include more time on tests, permission to use computers instead of handwriting classwork, or specialized tools such as writing grips for pencils or textured paper.

Also in 1990, a 1975 law called the Education for All Handicapped Children Act was expanded and renamed the Individuals with Disabilities Education Act (IDEA). This law established that students with physical or learning disabilities must be given appropriate accommodations for their disability that do not cost the parents anything; this ensures that the accommodations are available even to students whose families live in poverty. IDEA requires an Individualized Education Program (IEP) to be put in place for all students with disabilities. The student's IEP team decides on which accommodations will best help the student succeed in a classroom with their nondisabled peers.

segregation. All of these things hinder students' right to a free and equal education.

Equal Education and Language Barriers

It is indisputable that non-English-speaking immigrants who have entered the United States legally have the same right as natural-born citizens to attend public schools. However, the controversy over equality in relation to documented immigrants focuses on whether public schools are required to provide them with bilingual education or are allowed to offer classes only in English. Advocates of bilingual education do not belittle the importance of learning English; on the contrary, they believe it is much easier to learn English when students can use their native language as well. Laura Ferriero of the Mexican American Legal Defense and Educational Fund argued that "educational experts, Latino and otherwise, will tell you that bilingual education, when implemented properly, is the most effective way of teaching limited-English-proficient students."[8] In addition, advocates point out that immigrant students need to learn other core subjects—including math, social studies, science, and history—as well as English. In a bilingual setting, students can still keep up with these subjects while they also learn English. According to this viewpoint, denying students bilingual education is the same as denying them an education equal to that received by native speakers of English.

Many people disagree with this reasoning and support English immersion, or English-only, education. Some who are opposed to bilingual education believe it slows down the process of learning English, which makes it more difficult for immigrant children to integrate into American society. These people believe immigrants must stop using their first language and speak only English in order to fully participate in society and that it is more important for immigrant children to learn English quickly than to learn any other subject. In the past, this theory was widespread, but an increasing number of educators are coming to the conclusion that bilingual education is beneficial for all students. As bilingual education has come to be seen more as a right than a privilege, some states have begun to require bilingual education

Many teachers who have worked with students whose first language is not English have found that bilingual classes can help them learn the material better.

A DOUBLE STANDARD

"To put it bluntly, bilingualism is often seen as 'good' when it's rich English speakers adding a language as a hobby or another international language, but 'bad' when it involves poor, minority, or indigenous groups adding English to their first language, even when the same two languages are involved."

– Claire Bowern, associate professor of linguistics at Yale University, who has been researching bilingualism for more than 15 years

Quoted in Valerie Strauss, "Why Is Bilingual Education 'Good' for Rich Kids but 'Bad' for Poor, Immigrant Students?," *Washington Post*, October 24, 2014. www.washingtonpost.com/news/answer-sheet/wp/2014/10/24/why-is-bilingual-education-good-for-rich-kids-but-bad-for-poor-immigrant-students/.utm_term=.8fc91b023d13.

in their schools, although the specifics of these programs vary from state to state. For example, in Alaska, schools that have at least eight students who speak a language other than English must offer bilingual classes. In most other states with bilingual education programs, the minimum number of students is 20. In Wisconsin, individual schools that do not have the required minimum number of students can combine students of the same native language group from multiple schools. However, bilingual education is not yet required by federal law, so as of 2019, only eight states have this requirement. In the future, court cases similar to the ones regarding segregation may take place to require American schools to offer bilingual education programs.

Equality Among Genders

Like racial minorities and immigrants, girls and women have sought equal access to education throughout American history. Historically, the education of girls and women has been secondary to that of boys and men. For centuries, women were thought to be intellectually inferior to men, and their education was considered unnecessary. Although girls were sometimes allowed to attend primary schools in colonial America, they were often told to go home if all the classroom seats were taken by male students.

Over time, the prohibition against teaching girls and women lessened, and female students began to demand more educational opportunities. By the mid-1800s, women had begun to replace men as teachers, largely because school districts realized they could pay women lower wages than they paid men. Moreover, women gained more independence as the Industrial Revolution led to a need for educated workers.

These changes inspired women to see themselves as worthy of the same rights that men took for granted. Although the law required girls as well as boys to attend school until they were at least 16, there was no law requiring colleges and universities to admit women. Along with fighting for the right to vote and own property, they fought for the right to attend these all-male schools. Battles for access were waged one school at a time, and the doors to many institutions were opened only after years of protesting policies that barred women from higher education. Eventually, the rising legal and social status of women in society added to the pressure on all-male colleges and universities to become coeducational. Meanwhile, many colleges for women opened, delivering an education equal to that available at all-male schools. By 1900, an estimated one-third of resident college and university students were women. Publicly funded schools

Women struggled to get the same access to higher education that men enjoyed, but they eventually succeeded. They could then pursue careers in fields that had traditionally been reserved for men, such as medicine and chemistry. Shown here are female medical students dissecting bodies around 1900.

were often the first to grant access to women, while some private schools argued that since they were independent from the state, they had the right to exclude women.

Even bigger changes were underway by the 1960s. The women's rights movement involved women examining and challenging gender inequality in many areas of American life, including the home, the workplace, and schools. The growing interest in equality for women compelled Congress to pass Title IX of the Education Amendment Act in 1972. Title IX made it illegal for educational programs, public or private, to discriminate on the basis of a person's sex if the programs received federal funds. For school systems, this meant that a Title IX officer would monitor each school, help programs achieve equality, and handle complaints of discrimination. If corrections were not made, federal funding was withdrawn. Some of the first programs to be affected were previously sex-segregated programs in health, vocational education, physical education, and higher levels of mathematics and science. Many people give credit to Title IX for the rapid advancement of women in higher education. By 1984, women earned 49 percent of all undergraduate college degrees, and by 2003 more women than men—51 percent—were graduating from college.

Some people believe Title IX is unnecessary today. They say times have changed and women are not discriminated against anymore—at least, not enough to justify a special law. Some even suggest that Title IX has no real effect because women's brains are structured in a way that makes them worse at science and math than men—a claim that has been repeatedly disproven by neurological and sociological studies—or that women are simply less interested in science, technology, engineering, and math (STEM). Others see these false claims as evidence of why Title IX is still important. According to cognitive scientist Maria Natasha Rajah, evidence suggests "that society and life experience play much larger roles in distinguishing the sexes than brain differences."[9] Advocates of gender equality in schools base their concerns on evidence that peers, teachers, administrators, and school boards treat girls and boys differently. For example, research conducted by the American Association of University Women (AAUW) indicates that girls face a persistent bias against them in textbooks, teachers, and tests. The AAUW and other similar organizations argue that favoritism toward boys and lower expectations for girls end up shortchanging girls in significant ways. They believe that these additional barriers for girls in school tend to reduce their self-esteem, diminish their academic achievement, and lower their aspirations for higher education and successful careers.

Many point out that part of the reason for the lower numbers of women in optional STEM classes is that girls are often not encouraged to take them when they are no longer required. Before Title IX, women were actively prevented from taking STEM courses. The Intercultural Development Research Association said in 2000 that "the enactment of Title IX 25 years ago removed many barriers to women and girls in the non-traditional fields of math and science, areas critical to their success in an increasingly technological world."[10] Without Title IX, many people believe it would be difficult to motivate school officials to make the changes necessary for girls to receive an education equal to that of boys.

Furthermore, Title IX has been crucial in giving sexual assault survivors access to a timely and fair investigation into the matter if they choose to report the assault to their college. This part of the law—and reports of its numerous violations by multiple colleges—has been in the news frequently since the start of the 21st century. With Title IX in place, sexual assault victims have the option to sue their school if these rights are violated.

Another effect of Title IX was to require schools to support students who are pregnant or have children. In the past, pregnant teens might have been expelled from school; today, while this is not allowed, some schools test the limits of the law by making it so hard for the student that they choose to drop out on their own. Some of the ways a school may do this include making it difficult or impossible to attend classes or complete classwork, banning them from participating in extracurricular activities, refusing to give them schedule accommodations to allow for things such as extra doctor's appointments or picking up their child from daycare, or pressuring them to either drop out or switch schools. All of these actions are a violation of the student's Title IX rights.

MAINTAINING EQUALITY

"First of all, there's still a lot of discrimination against women, plain and simple, in all areas of education … We also need Title IX to make sure we don't slide back and lose progress."

– Marcia D. Greenberger, copresident of the National Women's Law Center

Quoted in Alexandra Gekas, "Q&A: Do We Still Need Title IX," Newsweek, June 22, 2007. www.newsweek.com/qa-do-we-still-need-title-ix-102153.

Programs That Support Equality

Gaining access to educational opportunities has been an important goal for excluded groups in America. However, the struggle for education without discrimination does not stop with the issue of who is able to attend school. Once inside the school doors, minority groups and women alike have also demanded changes in traditional curricula and educational policies.

Another area that has undergone adjustments is athletics, where girls' sports have long been treated as less important than boys' sports. Although Title IX has received much media attention in relation to its impact on athletic programs, federal sanctions against schools that fail to follow the law have not been substantial, and the few sanctions that have been put in place remain highly controversial in the media and American public opinion.

Those who oppose Title IX often argue that the regulations are unnecessary and extreme. They point to increasing opportunities in society for girls and women that have already reduced the gender gap. The most vocal critics of Title IX tend to be male athletes and coaches who argue that requiring male and female athletic opportunities to be proportionately equal is excessive and actually discriminates against male students. T.J. Kerr, wrestling coach at California State University, Bakersfield, claimed, "School administrators believe that they must achieve proportionality. Many are unable, because of budget constraints, to add female sports programs, so these administrators drop male programs or 'cap' sports by dropping [male athletes]. Both of these approaches to achieving 'gender equity' are wrong."[11] This view is widespread, but studies have proven it false. For example, in the early 2000s, the U.S. General Accounting Office—now called the Government Accountability Office (GAO)—found that "over 70 percent of schools added opportunities for women and did not cut back on any opportunities for men."[12] Another GAO report, this one from 2007, "found that while women's participation rates in college sports were increasing at a faster rate than men, the percentage of men playing sports still exceeded their share of enrollment, even as the numbers of women outstrip men on campus."[13] This shows that while men's sports are not being cut and Title IX has improved access to sports for women, a large gender gap remains. According to Marcia D. Greenberger, copresident of the National Women's Law Center, in cases where schools have cut men's sports teams, it is generally due to declining interest in the sport itself rather than a result of attempts to provide more opportunities for women.

Title IX has been an important part of giving girls equal opportunities to play sports, but experts say there is still more work to be done in this area.

Other critics of Title IX claim, again, that boys and girls are naturally different. Athletic programs should not be forced to provide equal opportunities for girls and women, according to this viewpoint, because they tend not to enjoy sports as much as boys and men do. As with other claims of biological differences between the sexes, this has been proven false in scientific studies. According to a study by the British Office for National Statistics, while it is true that more boys than girls play sports, "boys and girls who do participate in sport enjoy it equally."[14] Experts say that rather than being attributable to biological differences, the reason for this gap in participation likely has to do with societal factors, such as the fact that professional sports

Fighting for Title IX Rights

Although many schools follow the rules outlined in Title IX, sometimes they are found guilty of violations. For example, in September 2017, the Albany *Times Union* reported that the University of Albany (UAlbany) in New York State had fewer sports opportunities available to women than to men. When the school's women's tennis program was cut just weeks after the athletes won their first America East title, the program's head coach, Gordon Graham, filed a complaint with the U.S. Department of Education. The department's Office for Civil Rights investigated the complaint and found that "the UAlbany athletic department had not provided equal participation opportunities to male and female athletes over the past three academic years, in violation of Title IX."[1] Despite the fact that Title IX clearly states that schools found to be in violation of the law will have federal funding withdrawn, the Department of Education did not give UAlbany any financial penalties. However, the school did pledge to redistribute its athletic department's budget to improve opportunities for female student athletes.

Numerous other complaints against schools across the country have been filed over the years. Marcia D. Greenberger noted that even when schools have women's sports teams, reports of discriminatory treatment include "second class fields, less coaching support, more inconvenient practice times, inferior uniforms, more travel, [and fewer] scholarships."[2] Students who feel that any of their Title IX rights have been violated can file their own report. Many colleges allow students to make an anonymous report that will then be investigated by school officials. Students in elementary and high schools can speak to a trusted adult, such as a teacher, and ask for help filing a report.

1. Leif Skodnick, "Feds: UAlbany Athletics in Violation of Title IX," *Times Union*, September 18, 2017. www.timesunion.com/sports/article/Feds-UAlbany-athletics-in-violation-of-Title-IX-12200960.php.
2. Quoted in Alexandra Gekas, "Q&A: Do We Still Need Title IX," *Newsweek*, June 22, 2007. www.newsweek.com/qa-do-we-still-need-title-ix-102153.

careers are frequently seen as more achievable for men than for women. This could lead boys to practice more with the goal of becoming professional players, while girls may see their sports involvement more as an enjoyable hobby, thus spending less time on it.

Other possible factors include girls "being nervous that others will judge them for not being very good; it might stem from appearance, where women and girls don't want to look hot, sweaty and jiggly while exercising because it's not an image we see enough in the media; or there may be fear of being judged for their priorities, for being active instead of doing their homework or seeing their friends."[15] While this study was done in the United Kingdom (UK), society's view of women in sports is very similar in the United States. Unlike biological factors, all of these social factors can be addressed and potentially changed, so revoking Title IX and allowing individual schools to decide whether to take sports opportunities away from girls and women would not be helpful, experts say.

American education has been marked by a long history of struggle over these two basic questions about equality in schooling: Who deserves the right to have access to educational opportunities, and what type of curricula, teaching methods, and policies constitute an equal education for all students? Although things have improved over the centuries, especially for people of color and women, students must still sometimes defend the rights they have been granted.

CHAPTER 2

Freedom of Expression

The right to free speech is a fundamental part of life in the United States; the First Amendment to the Constitution guarantees it for all citizens. The right to "speak" actually implies the broader right of free expression. The First Amendment protects not only written or spoken words, but also what the Supreme Court calls "expressive conduct," or actions that do not literally involve speaking or writing yet nonetheless send a message. Freedom of expression for students can include personal appearance—hair length, clothing, body piercings, and tattoos—as well as classroom essays, student assembly presentations, and online journals or blogs.

Freedom of expression can be controversial both in and out of schools. Important questions have been debated for decades: Can hate speech be considered free speech? Do dress codes and uniforms give students a better learning environment or stifle their creativity? How much control should institutions such as schools have over the people who belong to them? When one person considers another person's freedom of expression to be offensive, whose viewpoint takes precedence? There are no simple answers to these questions, and many cases regarding free speech have been heard by the courts—and will likely continue to be heard in the future. A student's civil liberty is weighed not only against the good of the community, but also against the educational mission of the school. This additional element sometimes makes free speech conflicts in education even more complicated than those in society in general.

The Pledge of Allegiance

Most schools start the day by having all students face the American flag and recite the Pledge of Allegiance. This tradition dates back to the 1920s, but the words "under God" were not added to the pledge until 1954. Some people defend this daily recitation, saying that it teaches children loyalty to and pride in their country. Many believe it shows respect not only to the government but also to the soldiers who have fought in past wars because of their belief in a free country, although the pledge does not explicitly mention soldiers. In an opinion letter published on the website Daily American, a woman named Allison Fiddler wrote, "Although after high school most students will not say the Pledge of Allegiance every day it is still important to have been raised knowing the importance of it and what it stands for, so that in their future they will keep patriotism with them."[16]

Since the 1920s, most American children have started their school day by saying the Pledge of Allegiance. However, this practice is not without controversy.

Others disagree that the pledge is necessary or even desirable. One of the most frequently cited reasons is that since separation of church and state is an important part of the U.S. government, people should not be required to pledge their allegiance to the Christian God. However, the pledge has inspired a major debate related to freedom of speech for students on more than religious grounds. Some believe that requiring children to recite a pledge they might not even understand is morally wrong. They argue that the pledge forces students to express a particular political viewpoint whether or not they agree with that viewpoint. Some people who support the pledge do not, at the same time, believe children should be punished if they choose not to recite it. A woman who identified herself as Tessa Lynn pointed out on Daily American,

> For an abundant number of students, actions speak louder than words, and they believe they can show their patriotism and love for their country in other ways that are more meaningful to them. This country was founded on the idea of freedom for all and requiring students to say the pledge would be the opposite [of freedom].[17]

Others oppose the pledge entirely and do not believe it should be said in schools. These people tend to believe that the United States does not embody the values recited in the pledge; as a woman named Kaitlyn Carney explained on Daily American, "With all of the issues present in today's society—from racial injustices to women's issues—are we really united as one nation and do we really have liberty and justice for all?"[18] Some students have been inspired not to say the Pledge of Allegiance by football player Colin Kaepernick, who began kneeling when the national anthem was played before games as a form of protest against racial injustice. In some cases, these students have been suspended for doing so and have successfully sued their schools for violating their rights.

Officially, the debate about whether or not to require students to recite the pledge was resolved in the 1943 Supreme Court case *West Virginia Board of Education v. Barnette*. At that time, students were expected to raise their right hands in salute at the beginning of the day while they recited the Pledge of Allegiance. Children of the Jehovah's Witness faith faced widespread persecution; their religion forbids them to pledge their loyalty to anything or anyone aside from God, so they refused to salute the flag. Some were expelled from school and threatened with being sent to reformatory schools for delinquent youth. When the suit protesting such treatment reached the Supreme Court, punishment for refusal to say the pledge was struck down as unconstitutional. Students today have the right to opt out of saluting and saying the pledge if it goes against their political or religious beliefs.

A VETERAN'S IDEA OF TRUE RESPECT

"I can tell you, speaking for three generations of my family, it is PRECISELY for ... [the] right to peacefully protest injustice, that we were willing to serve ... Want to respect the American flag? Then respect the ideals for which it stands. Bullying language ... [isn't] among them."

– Michael Sands, veteran of the
United States Army Special Forces

Quoted in Paul Szoldra and Christopher Woody, "Soldiers Speak Out on Kaepernick: His Protest 'Makes Him More American Than Anyone,'" Business Insider, September 25, 2017, www.businessinsider.com/veterans-colin-kaepernick-september-25-2017.

However, *West Virginia Board of Education v. Barnette* did not end the conflict over the issue. Some schools chose not to follow the decision and continued to punish or stigmatize students who refused to stand and recite the pledge. In his research for the First Amendment Center, law professor David L. Hudson Jr. reported, "In March 1998, a 13-year-old Jehovah's Witness in a Seattle middle school was forced to stand outside in the rain for 15 minutes for refusing to say the pledge. In April 1998, a 16-year-old student in San Diego was forced to serve detention for her failure to recite the pledge."[19] Hudson also noted that a surge of patriotism after the September 11, 2001, terrorist attacks fueled new efforts to require all students to recite the pledge to demonstrate their loyalty to the United States. This rationale makes some Americans uneasy: Forcing children to "prove" their loyalty through mandatory oaths strikes many as an erosion of First Amendment protections, especially since no such loyalty test is required of the general public. Others argue that national loyalty must be instilled at an early age to ensure that all children will grow up to be good citizens.

As *West Virginia Board of Education v. Barnette* ruled, no matter what their reasons are, students are legally protected if they choose to sit or stand quietly during the Pledge of Allegiance. However, students who do so are expected to respect their fellow classmates who do choose to say the pledge. For this reason, it is not considered a violation of a student's right not to say the pledge if they are punished for talking, moving around, or otherwise being disruptive during the pledge.

Expression Through Clothing

Another controversy over students' freedom of expression concerns school dress codes and mandatory uniforms. Do the clothing and appearance of students fall under the umbrella of the educational mission of schools or the freedom of expression of individual students? Compelling arguments have been made on both sides of the issue.

Sometimes dress-code conflict is a matter of getting schools to adjust to current fashion trends, which come and go. Sometimes, however, dress-code conflict is a reflection of wider social rebellion or tests of authority. In the 1960s and 1970s, for example, the baby boomer youth culture encouraged boys and men to wear their hair long as a form of rebellion as well as a fashion trend. Since short hair had been the norm in previous decades, students and school codes clashed, and the dispute ended up in court.

In numerous legal cases, the courts upheld the right of school administrators to regulate the length of male students' hair. For example, in the 1972 case *Karr v. Schmidt*, Fifth Circuit judge Lewis R. Morgan argued that a student's right to hair length is less important than the school's intention to eliminate classroom distraction, prevent violence between long- and short-haired students, and eliminate health and safety hazards caused by long hairstyles. However, some judges wrote dissenting opinions indicating that such a regulation infringed on the rightful liberty of students because hair length can be a symbol of group

Some schools have length restrictions on boys' hair; some say it cannot be below the shoulders, while others say it cannot be below the ears. The courts have ruled that this is not an infringement of a student's rights.

affinity as well as nonconformity—in other words, it can be a personal and political statement.

Debates about student clothing are often related to conflicts over sexual and racial discrimination. For example, in April 2018, a 17-year-old Florida student named Lizzy Martinez chose not to wear a bra to school because she had gotten a sunburn over the weekend and the bra irritated her skin. She wore a loose shirt that did not show off her breasts, but she was called to the principal's office and told by school administrators that she had to cover up somehow because she was in violation of the dress code and male students were laughing at her. According to the *New York Times*, which reported the story, both of these statements were false; the school's published dress code did not say girls were required to wear bras, and Martinez said she had not noticed anyone laughing at her. Martinez agreed to put on an undershirt, but officials told her that was not enough, so they required her to put on adhesive bandages. Martinez was humiliated by this treatment and found the bandages painful to wear. Martinez did not take the case to court, but more than 30 girls protested on her behalf the following week by not wearing bras to school. While the school claimed its intention was to protect other students' learning environment from disruption, law professor Meredith Harbach pointed out that Martinez was the only one who ended up dealing with a disruption in her school day—not from her lack of a bra, but from the officials' attempt to enforce what they felt was a moral standard.

The question of what schools are allowed to regulate in regard to dress codes is a tricky one. Most people agree that a dress code in and of itself is not a problem; after all, workplaces have dress codes as well. Some offices require employees to wear suits to work, while others have less strict dress codes that simply prohibit offensive clothing, such as shirts with sexually sugges-tive pictures or phrases. At minimum, no matter where they are, people must cover areas of the body that would be considered indecent if they were exposed. Churches, courts, and other public places may also have their own type of dress code, such as a ban on shorts, and can ask people to leave if they are not dressed appropriately.

Dress Codes and Religion

In most schools, head coverings such as hats and hoodies are not allowed. However, one important exception to this rule is the hijab–the headscarf Muslim women wear as a sign of their faith. In the United States, freedom of religion is protected, so Muslim students are allowed to wear the hijab to school. However, there has been a worldwide rise in Islamophobia (fear of Muslims and the Islamic religion) since the highly visible terrorist attacks on the World Trade Center and the Pentagon on September 11, 2001. This has led some American schools or individual teachers to try to force Muslim girls to take their hijab off during school hours, which is a violation of their rights. For example, in November 2017, a teacher at a Virginia school pulled his student's hijab off her head. The teacher claimed that he thought the student was wearing a hoodie over her hijab and was trying to pull only the hood off her head, but he was still placed on leave by school administrators.

Hijabs are not the only religious accessory that students have fought to be allowed to wear. At various times, students have protested bans on things such as necklaces featuring the Christian cross, traditional Native American dress, and rosaries.

Dress codes are meant to keep students' attention on the learning environment, so clothes that are distracting, offensive, or likely to provoke violence can be banned. Examples of dress code rules that do not violate a student's right to free expression include limits on gang-related clothing (including specific colors in areas with high gang activity); bans on shirts with words or images regarding illegal drug use, violence, or sexually explicit situations; and bans on clothing that is too tight, too short, or too revealing, regardless of gender. An issue only arises with school dress codes if they are discriminatory in some way. The American Civil Liberties Union (ACLU) explained that "while dress codes may specify *types* of attire that are acceptable, these requirements should not differ based on students' sex or their race."[20]

Many girls have reported being targeted for dress code violations if their bra strap is showing. There has been a wave of backlash against policies such as these, which many say unfairly make female students responsible for their male classmates' reactions to them.

In the past few years, dress code discrimination against girls has been highly visible in the media, including news reports and social media posts. According to the ACLU, "Dress codes are frequently unevenly enforced against girls for wearing clothing that is considered a 'distraction' to boys in the classroom—reinforcing stereotypes about how 'good girls' dress and privileging boys' ability to concentrate over girls' comfort and ability to learn."[21] In many schools, girls can be disciplined for showing their collarbones, shoulders, or knees, while boys are typically not held to this same standard. Furthermore, some students have reported that in their schools, the dress code rules are enforced more strictly for black girls than for either white girls or male students. Some policies also directly target black students in subtle ways. For example, in March 2017, two 15-year-old students from Boston "were barred from the prom, taken out of extracurricular activities and threatened with suspension if they wouldn't remove their braided hair extensions. The Massachusetts Attorney General ordered the school to reverse their policy."[22] This type of policy unfairly targets black girls, as they are more likely to wear braided extensions and white girls do not receive the same type of treatment for having naturally long hair.

Taking a Political Stance

Resistance to dress codes sometimes goes hand in hand with other forms of student protest. *Tinker v. Des Moines Independent Community School District* was a 1969 case involving students who wore armbands to school in protest of the Vietnam War. The students' right to conduct this silent method of protest was upheld by the courts, largely because it was found that their expression did not disrupt class work or otherwise interfere with the educational operation of the school. For this reason, schools cannot forbid students to wear clothing with political messages on them, as long as those messages do not incite violence.

Students have also taken a more active role in political protest. For example, in the late 1960s and early 1970s, college students across the United States staged sit-ins and walkouts to protest America's involvement in the Vietnam War. In 2018, high school students gained national attention for their protests against gun violence. After a student named Nikolas Cruz opened fire on Marjory Stoneman Douglas High School in Parkland, Florida, on February 14, 2018, students across the country rose up to demand a change in current gun laws. On March 14, 2018, thousands of students walked out of class for 17 minutes—one minute for each person killed in the Parkland shooting—as a way of both paying tribute to the Parkland victims and making their feelings about gun laws known.

Some schools supported their students by allowing them to walk out without punishment, but others threatened detention or suspension for those who participated. According to the ACLU, "Because the law in most places requires students

THE RESPONSIBILITY OF SCHOOLS

"Schools stand in what's known as loco parentis (in place of parents), so we don't simply release our students [without supervision] … You know it's finding that balance between people realizing that this is civil disobedience—some of them may get punished for walking out—but making sure that they're ensuring the safety of their own lives."

– Francisco Negron, chief legal officer at the National School Boards Association

Quoted in Sarah Gray, "Everything You Need to Know About the April 20 National School Walkout," TIME, April 19, 2018. time.com/5238216/national-school-walkout-april-20/.

to go to school, schools can discipline you for missing class. But what they can't do is discipline you more harshly because of the political nature of or the message behind your action."[23] In other words, if someone would not be suspended for missing one class under different circumstances, they cannot be suspended for missing one class due to their participation in a political protest.

Student free expression has been met with mixed reactions. Those who defend student speech argue that young people should have the same rights as adults. They warn against suppressing the views of a substantial group of people who contribute important perspectives on a variety of issues. For these advocates, free speech is an essential tool for teaching young people to participate in a democratic nation. On the other hand, those who favor limiting student speech tend to believe that young people are not yet able to meet the responsibilities of full citizenship. To them, absolute free speech can disrupt the cooperative environment necessary to provide young people with a quality education. Many adults who disapproved of the student walkouts stated their view that student protests should take place after school or on the weekends rather than disrupting class for all students, even those who chose not to take part in the protest.

Thousands of students across the United States participated in two school walkouts in 2018 to protest gun violence—one on March 14 and the other on April 20. The first commemorated the Parkland victims and the second marked 19 years since the Columbine school shooting, which had previously been the worst school shooting in U.S. history.

RESPECTING STUDENT PROTESTS

"When you have ... students come and talk that maturely and that astutely, to try to squash that and to try to quell that is just not right and our thinking as educators needs to change, and we have to respect student voice."

– Paul Casseri, superintendent of Lewiston-Porter Central Schools in New York State, discussing why he believes students should not be punished for staging walkout protests

Quoted in George Richert, "Suspensions Given to Niagara Wheatfield Students Who Walked Out of School," WIVB, June 4, 2019. www.wivb.com/news/local-news/suspensions-given-to-niagara-wheatfield-students-who-walked-out-of-school/2052606166?fbclid=IwAR0R521XeqvXqeM68PDCCsbPfeGAsHmmBEbYwWZC9sxDrytt6ov7q6\jM

Freedom of Speech on the Internet

With the rise of the internet, free speech in schools has become more complicated. Most people agree that schools have the right to make certain rules regarding the use of personal devices on campus; for example, they may make a rule that cell phones cannot be used during school hours, even if the person is in a hallway or study hall. Schools also have the right to make rules regarding computers that belong to the school. They can restrict access to certain websites and monitor what the user is doing by installing software that records things such as browsing history. Schools are also allowed to monitor what students post privately on their social media accounts; however, the ACLU noted that in this case, the school district "must let you and your parents know, allow you to see the information it has collected about your social media activity, and delete it when you leave the district or turn 18."[24] The ACLU warns, however, that if a school does not have a social media monitoring policy in place, students' public social media posts are not protected, as information that is voluntarily made public on the internet is available for anyone to find. Students should be mindful of their accounts' privacy settings and of what they are posting online in general.

Students generally have the right to make their own opinions known on social media, and they cannot be punished for it even if the school disagrees with their opinion. However, there are limits to this freedom of speech. Just as someone is not protected offline for encouraging violence or inciting panic—the common example is that someone cannot yell "Fire!" in a crowded theater—a student can be disciplined by their school if something they post online is considered a substantial disruption. The ACLU explained:

> *Your speech is a substantial disruption when it encourages violations of school rules, illegal activities, or it risks causing a big interference with the education of other students. For example, threats to other students or your teachers using social media will likely be considered a substantial disruption ...*

*If you use your own device and accounts outside of school hours
and your posts are not related to school, your school cannot discipline you for those posts. But if you post something on your own
device or account outside of school hours that creates a "substantial
disruption" to the school environment, your school can discipline
you. For example ... threats of violence or harassment directed at
classmates or school officials can get you in trouble, even if you post
them on your own time and on your own device.[25]*

Punishment for out-of-school internet posts that cause
a substantial disruption was upheld in the 2000 court case
J.S. v. Bethlehem Area School District, when a student who identified himself as J.S. created a website that made negative comments about his principal and a specific teacher. It was considered a substantial disruption because J.S. drew a picture of
the teacher's severed head and asked people to give him money
so he could hire someone to kill the teacher. Students can also
be punished if a post provides evidence that they have broken
school rules; for example, a picture of someone drinking alcohol
at school can be grounds for punishment even if the picture was
posted from a home computer.

Internet Restriction Policies in Public Schools

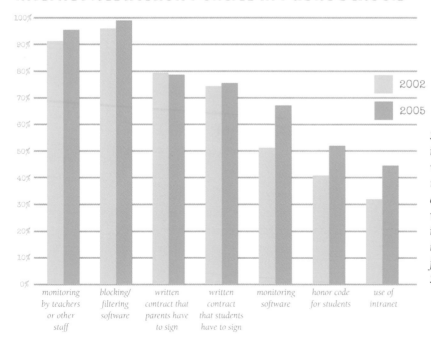

Schools are increasingly using various methods of restricting students' access to certain websites, as this information from the National Center for Education Statistics shows.

The ACLU noted that cyberbullying may be considered a substantial disruption to another student's educational environment, so students who harass classmates through social media may be disciplined by the school. Some schools have made rules prohibiting students from posting anything mean or intimidating online, whether they do so in school or at home. Some people support these rules, saying that they protect students and teachers from online bullies. Others oppose them because they fear schools will be able to punish any statement they do not agree with as long as they can claim the post was intimidating.

Student Rights in Private Schools

The rights of private school students are not the same as those of public school students. While public schools are funded by the government, private schools are funded mainly by the tuition parents pay to send their children there. When students are enrolled, they typically sign a contract with the school promising to abide by the school's code of conduct. This contract overrides the students' constitutional rights. This means that if the school has a policy saying every student must stand for the Pledge of Allegiance, it is not a violation of a student's rights if they are punished for sitting.

Codes of conduct vary from school to school; for example, a Catholic school may require students to pray in class, while a nonreligious private school may forbid students from doing so. Students who have questions about what they are and are not allowed to do at their school must read their own school's code of conduct.

Private schools handle student rights issues much differently than public schools handle them. However, this does not mean private schools have no rules at all regarding student rights; as in public schools, it is illegal for staff to hurt students, and schools are not allowed to deny students entry based on race. Additionally, each state has its own rules regarding private schools and how they can and cannot differ from public schools in the state.

Controversy arises when students are punished for things they post online outside of school hours and the punishment is out of proportion to what was written. According to *The Atlantic*:

> *In 2012, after a Minnesota student wrote a Facebook post saying a hall monitor was "mean" to her, she was forced to turn over her Facebook password to school administrators—in the presence of a sheriff's deputy. The school made an out-of-court settlement with the student, who was represented by the ACLU.*[26]

This was considered an overreach of the school's authority because the student had not threatened anyone and had made the post on her private account. In another instance in which the court ruled against a school's action, a Pennsylvania high school student was cut from the junior varsity cheerleading team in 2017 because she made a social media post over the weekend that contained a swear word.

However, even when school officials determine that a social media post causes a substantial disruption, many question how far the case can be taken. For instance, in 2017, Instagram posts were made by a student at a San Francisco, California, high school that involved racist and violent depictions of several black female students and a black basketball coach. The student who made the posts was suspended—and so were four other students who "liked" and commented on the posts. While the original poster's suspension and possible expulsion were not challenged, a lawsuit was filed on behalf of the other four students, claiming that the meaning of an internet "like" is too unclear to determine and that it does not show enough involvement in the incident to warrant punishment.

The question that is still being decided is how much involvement schools should be allowed to have in students' home lives. Some argue that since a student represents their school, the school should be allowed to discipline actions that do not portray the school in a good light. Legal analysts Mike Hiestand and Mark Goodman argued against this view, saying, "For many high school students today, the opportunity to express themselves in a school-sponsored medium without administrative censorship has been all but eliminated. The Internet has created a meaningful alternative."[27] To critics such as Hiestand and Goodman, extending schools' jurisdiction over student speech to the internet is a violation of the civil liberties of young people. This aspect of the debate over student free speech continues to grow more complex as technology becomes more deeply ingrained in today's society.

The debate about whether limits on free expression can be justified extends far beyond school campuses. As the above examples show, censorship of speech and other student expression occurs for a number of reasons, from the trivial to the personal to the political. Political speech may get the most attention, but court decisions have shown that speech does not have to be overtly inflammatory in order to be restricted. Regardless of the reasons, the infringement of free expression both in and out of school continues to be a controversial issue.

CHAPTER 3

Freedom of the School Press

Freedom of the press has always been an important quality to Americans. In 1787, Thomas Jefferson wrote, "The basis of our governments being the opinion of the people, the very first object should be to keep that right; and were it left to me to decide whether we should have a government without newspapers, or newspapers without government, I should not hesitate a moment to prefer the latter."[28] However, as with other issues, many people disagree on whether the rights given to adult citizens extend to students. Some believe that since a school newspaper is created on a school campus, the same limits should be placed on it that are placed on freedom of expression in schools. Others argue that censoring student journalists goes against one of the founding principles of the country. Supporters of a free student press tend to believe that students need and deserve avenues for editorial, creative, and journalistic training just as much as the general public does.

Does Sponsorship Excuse Censorship?

The first student newspaper in the United States was the *Student Gazette*, started in 1777 at Penn Charter School in Philadelphia, Pennsylvania. This newspaper, however, was run by groups of students working on their own rather than by the school itself. This model changed when journalism became an optional class in high schools in 1912, and soon journalism classes were expected to produce a school newspaper as part of the learning experience.

This development changed the nature of the student press. Historian Nicholas D. Kristof explained:

> With school support, student newspapers became more professional—in the sense that the writing was better and that they looked more like commercial newspapers. But they also became more like house public relations newsletters, with the expectation that they would propagandize for the school and cover only "good news." The result was a tension between increased professionalism, which implied aggressive, skeptical reporting, and the tendency of administrators to see the school newspaper as a public relations tool.[29]

When student journalists tried to report content beyond school social and athletic activities—for instance, publishing editorials criticizing school policies or writing about local or national politics—they began to encounter resistance by teachers or school administrators. In some instances, school officials refused permission to print what they saw as offensive or controversial material. Until the mid-20th century, it was generally accepted that administrators and teachers had the authority to review student publications and remove sensitive or controversial material.

Conflicts over censorship in student newspapers increased as a result of the political unrest among students during the 1960s. In response to censorship of their official school newspapers, students sometimes started "underground" papers that they produced off the school campus. This independence allowed them to report content and express views that school officials condemned. Students in Madison, Wisconsin, for example, went off their high school campus to produce the underground newspaper *Links* in the late 1960s. Their mission statement expressed their desire for more freedom of speech:

> We started [Links] because the regular press just doesn't meet the needs of young people throughout the state. The issues which directly affect us are ignored by established press and "official" high school papers ... Links is an attempt ... to build our own means of communication, our own media, controlled by us, and through which our ideas, beliefs, and experiences can be freely and fully expressed.[30]

During the 1960s, many people—especially students, such as this group protesting at the University of Michigan—were strongly against American involvement in the Vietnam War. Some schools censored political content, so students began publishing their own newspapers, which they frequently distributed on campus.

PICK YOUR BATTLES

"Fighting for a free student press is a worthy endeavor. But the truth is, some censorship fights are worthier than others. Do you really want to go to battle over the right to use a four-letter word? Or the right to publish a … rumor-filled gossip column? … There are no hard rules for determining when a fight is worth the time and effort involved, but the question should always be asked."

– Student Press Law Center

"Responding to Censorship." Student Press Law Center, accessed on March 15, 2019. splc.org/responding-to-censorship/.

The tension between administrators seeking more control over school newspapers and student reporters seeking greater freedom continues to fuel the debate about the appropriate degree of freedom of the press in education. Struggles over the issue have resulted in landmark Supreme Court cases that define the legal boundaries of student press freedom. Legal cases have defined the rights of the student press at both the high school and college or university levels. Moreover, now that the internet has become a popular forum for expression in America, the courts are beginning to address the freedom of student online publications.

Protections and Limitations

Before the 1980s, public high school administrators were limited by the Supreme Court decision in *Tinker v. Des Moines* when they wanted to suppress the free speech of students. Although the case involved a particular form of expression—displaying a symbol of protest—that was quite different from publishing articles, it greatly affected the world of student journalism. For almost 20 years after the decision, *Tinker v. Des Moines* set the standard for recognizing students' right to free expression, including the right to publish their observations and opinions in student newspapers. It was not until 1988 that the journalistic rights of high school students were definitively set apart from those of college students in the landmark Supreme Court case *Hazelwood School District v. Kuhlmeier*.

The original lawsuit was initiated in 1983 by three students who had graduated from Hazelwood East High School just outside of St. Louis, Missouri. The students had worked on the year's final issue of the school newspaper, the *Spectrum*, in which they featured a special "teen issue" section that included an article describing several students' experiences with pregnancy and another article discussing the impact of divorce on students at Hazelwood.

The *Spectrum* was written and edited by a journalism class as part of the school's curriculum. The newspaper's policy at the time was for the journalism teacher to submit the page proofs to the school's principal for approval before publication. When

Hazelwood principal Robert Reynolds read the pregnancy and divorce stories in the page proofs of this particular issue, he decided to delete the two pages of the *Spectrum* that contained those articles. He objected to the pregnancy story because he feared the pregnant students, although not named in the article, could be identified from other details in the text. In addition to his desire to protect their privacy, he also felt that the article's discussion of sexual activity and birth control was unsuitable for younger students. He believed the article about divorce needed to be censored because it contained sharp criticism from a student about her father. Reynolds believed the student's parents should have been given an opportunity to respond to her remarks or to consent to their publication. Reynolds's superiors agreed with his decision.

The three student members of the *Spectrum* staff filed suit against the Hazelwood School District and school officials, and the case was appealed all the way to the Supreme Court. *Hazelwood* was decided on January 13, 1988. In striking contrast to decisions handed down since *Tinker*, the Supreme Court ruled in favor of the principal who censored the controversial stories. *Hazelwood* now allows school officials to edit and censor school publications that are produced as part of a class. As long as the school has no additional policy that expands the freedom of its student press, administrators can make the final decisions about what will or will not be published in a school newspaper. However, limiting free expression is allowed only if school officials determine that the censored content is without educational value or merit. In other words, principals and teachers must not prevent an article from being published merely because they disagree with a student's viewpoint.

Other Controversies

Administrators have used methods other than outright censorship to gain more control over school newspapers. In some instances, principals have seized all copies of a newspaper after it has been published in order to prevent its distribution. One of the first post-*Hazelwood* cases brought this issue to the attention of the American public. The incident took place after students

Shown here is Robert Reynolds holding a copy of the Spectrum *after the Supreme Court's* Hazelwood *decision.*

published an article in an Ohio high school newspaper alleging that the Wooster City School Board violated its own underage drinking policy by giving preferential treatment to athletes caught drinking. Wooster High School's principal seized all copies of the newspaper after it was printed. His concern was that the article quoted a student-athlete who admitted to drinking, which could have negative consequences for the student.

Members of the paper filed a lawsuit, claiming the confiscation of the papers amounted to "prior restraint" of speech, or preventative censorship, in violation of the First Amendment. The district court determined that the policy on student media established by the Wooster City School Board gave it the right to use prior restraint and therefore prevent distribution of the newspaper. Before the case went to court, the school board's policy on student media described "publications which are not protected by the right of free expression because they violate the rights of others. Such unprotected materials are those which ... libel any specific person or persons."[31] Since the Wooster High School principal was worried about the athlete's reputation, the court supported his confiscation of the newspapers.

The 2003 *Draudt v. Wooster City School District Board of Education* decision also further clarified the distinction between "public" and "nonpublic" forum publications in relation to school environments. Legally, a public forum is defined as

Important distinctions separate how student newspapers should be treated based on how they are created. For example, newspapers created as part of a class are treated differently than those created as part of a club after school.

Press Passes

A press pass is a special card that identifies someone as a member of a media organization who is at an event to report the news. These cards distinguish members of the actual press from people claiming to be reporters in order to get free admission to certain events. The Student Press Law Center recommends that even student publications should issue press passes so their journalists do not get turned away from important events.

In March 2019, the newspaper of the University at Buffalo, the *Spectrum*, left the front page of one of its issues completely blank. In the following issue, a letter from the editor-in-chief explained that this was because *Spectrum* reporters had been turned away from an important school-funded campus event by the president of the Student Association (SA), Gunnar Haberl, and the coordinator of the event, Elise Helou. Helou explained that she had made the decision because she did not believe it was fair to let the press in for free when the event was sold out and many other people had already been turned away. According to the *Spectrum*, this was a violation of the freedom of the school press. The article explained, "By turning us away, the SA turned you away. We represent you, the students. We're your voice on campus. We're the university's historical record."[1]

The editor-in-chief admitted that the paper had not applied for a press pass for the event, but went on to say,

> We admit, our editors should have done that. But editors have forgotten in the past without being turned away. We cover many events all over the city without press passes. On campus, we are all students, we know each other …

> And when it comes down to it, a press pass is a formality. It's useful to separate real press from outsiders. Gunnar knows who we are. He knows what we do. He should have helped us, not blocked the door.[2]

While some people agreed that turning the reporters away showed disregard for the freedom of the press, many others noted that the First Amendment does not require journalists to be allowed into an event, especially without having previously applied for a press pass to guarantee their spot.

1. Hannah Stein, "Letter from the Editor," *Spectrum*, March 14, 2019. www.ubspectrum.com/article/2019/03/letter-from-the-editor-19.
2. Stein, "Letter from the Editor."

a place that is generally used by the public for speech-related purposes. In the school setting, a newspaper is a public forum when the administration has given student editors the authority to make their own content decisions. The government is not allowed to restrict the content of speech in a public forum unless it can show that a compelling governmental interest is at stake; for example, secret military strategies can be censored if revealing them could threaten national security. Since student publications virtually never interfere with the government in this way, there is little risk of them being censored on these grounds.

The Supreme Court's *Hazelwood* decision declared that high school newspapers that are produced in journalism classes are nonpublic forum publications because editorial decisions are ultimately made by the journalism teacher or the school principal. However, in the *Draudt* case, the Court developed criteria that separated newspapers produced in a class from newspapers produced in an after-school club. Extracurricular newspapers were considered a "limited public forum," as they have some history of student-based editorial decisions. Publications produced in a limited public forum have more First Amendment protections than nonpublic forum newspapers. *Draudt* is an important case because it determined that high school publications classified as public or limited public forums are protected by the much higher *Tinker*-based standard rather than the *Hazelwood* standard. This means that, in order to censor these publications, school officials must show that the material is either illegal or substantially disruptive to the school. For this reason, students who want to criticize school or political policies generally create their own publication that does not rely on help from the school and is therefore not subject to the strict *Hazelwood* standard. In the past, unofficial student publications might be produced off-campus and distributed on or near the school grounds. Today, students are more likely to create a website or blog, as these require much less money to maintain.

The Supreme Court's *Hazelwood* decision dealt only with high school student publications. While a few college and university officials have tried to extend the *Hazelwood* standard to apply to their campuses, courts have consistently ruled against

What to Do About Censorship

In an article for the Student Press Law Center, attorney advocate Adam Goldstein gave students advice on what to do if they find themselves censored in ways that are outside the rules set by the various court cases that have ruled on this issue:

1. **Appeal internally.** *That is, figure out who in the administration is censoring you; why they're censoring you; and appeal that decision the way you would appeal any other decision—by asking for a meeting with that individual, and if that doesn't work, his or her supervisor. At a public high school, this ends with the school board, and that's the last stop for internal appeals. Private high schools and colleges might have a different setup, but there will eventually be a final decision from the institution.*

2. **Appeal to the public.** *Every school, public or private, answers to the public in one way or another, whether it's through the elected officials of a school board or the marketplace for tuition dollars. Going public can be an extremely powerful tool to convince schools to do the right thing and respect your expression rights.*

3. **Appeal to a court.** *If you have a strong case and public pressure doesn't do the trick, there's the option to seek legal remedies, of course.*

Here's the thing: you aren't obligated to do all of these things because you choose to do one of them, and you don't have to have a case that would be a viable lawsuit in order to be in the right. You can still speak up and call out the school for doing the wrong thing, even if, at the end of the day, you don't have the time or interest in making a federal case out of it.[1]

1. Adam Goldstein, "From the Hotline: What Do I Do When I'm Censored?," Student Press Law Center, September 4, 2014. splc.org/2014/09/hotline-wrongly-censored/.

the power of administrators to censor school-sponsored student expression in higher education.

Freedom of the Press in the Digital Age

One of the first cases to consider whether the liberal *Tinker* standard or the more conservative *Hazelwood* standard should govern student speech on the internet was the 1998 *Beussink v. Woodland R-IV School District* case. Brandon Beussink was a junior at Woodland High School in Marble Hill, Missouri. He made a website that expressed criticism of the school's principal and a teacher using what the court described as "crude and vulgar language."[32] When the homepage came to the attention of principal Yancy Poorman, he demanded that Beussink remove the page, which he did. Nevertheless, Poorman suspended the student for 10 days. The lengthy suspension caused Beussink to fail all of his junior-year classes because of the school's absenteeism policy.

Beussink took the school district to court, where presiding district judge Rodney Sippel ruled that Beussink's homepage was not subject to *Hazelwood* standards because the publication was created off campus. Furthermore, using the *Tinker* standard, the court found that the homepage had not caused disruption at the school and therefore was protected. Sippel wrote, "Disliking or being upset by the content of a student's speech is not an acceptable justification for limiting student speech under *Tinker*."[33]

As with freedom of expression, the internet makes it tricky for schools to set and enforce regulations on the press. In 2015, 18-year-old SaraRose Martin of Fauquier High School in Virginia wrote an article for her school's newspaper, the *Falconer*, about a drug-related activity called dabbing. The school's principal, Clarence Burton III, said it could not run in the *Falconer*, as he was concerned that students would learn about dabbing from the article and try it themselves.

According to *Hazelwood*, Burton was not violating Martin's freedom of speech by censoring her article. However, the issue was important to her. She said she wrote the article because "I was just interested in exactly what it was and exactly what

Like many professional newspapers, such as the New York Times,
some student newspapers today have an online version.

the effects of it were … I wanted my peers to know what they were doing."[34]

For this reason, she approached *Fauquier Now*, an online-only publication that reported news from around Fauquier County. The editor-in-chief decided to run Martin's piece, giving it a much wider audience than it would have had if it had appeared only in the *Falconer*.

WRITING DOES NOT EQUAL ENCOURAGEMENT

"There's obviously a difference between exposing people to information and exposing them to a drug … They didn't enclose drugs in the publication."

– Frank LoMonte, executive director of the Student Press Law Center, on why he disagreed with Clarence Burton III's censorship

Quoted in Moriah Balingit, "A Principal Yanked a Drug Article from a Student Newspaper, so It Ran Online," *Washington Post*, April 5, 2015, www.washingtonpost.com/local/education/a-principal-yanked-a-drug-article-from-a-student-newspaper-so-it-ran-online/2015/04/05/26588063-d4ce-11e4-ab77-2646ee1a4c7/story.html?utm_term=6ff9e6bcbd75.

Neither Burton nor Martin broke any laws or school rules with their actions, but the case is interesting because of how easily the internet gave Martin a way around her school's censorship. David Jeck, Fauquier County's schools superintendent, said that although he is aware this option is open to students, he does not intend to stop censorship of school papers when the faculty believes it is necessary. He explained, "We know very well that the kids have access to a thousand times more information than they would in the Falconer newspaper … That doesn't mean we have to be part of that."[35] While some agree that the school's role is to protect students, others believe censoring well-written, factual articles about topics that affect the student population only encourages students to get their news from other sources that may not be as accurate. In their view, the school should be encouraging students to do good research on controversial topics rather than suppressing them altogether.

Whether direct or indirect, censorship is a hot-button issue that continues to generate strong feelings in Americans. The issue of how much press freedom should be permitted in a democracy is further complicated when the reporters and editors are students and their work appears in an educational context. Americans cherish freedom of speech, but they also strive to protect individual privacy and educational integrity. Decisions about the freedom of student media publications are tricky when these competing interests collide.

CHAPTER 4

Freedom of Religion

Like freedom of speech and freedom of the press, freedom of religion is a fundamental principal upon which the United States was founded. The first people to come to settle in what is now Plymouth, Massachusetts, left England to escape religious persecution, and people have interpreted parts of the First Amendment to guarantee the separation of church and state. This means the government cannot set laws based on the principles of any religion, and it is an important part of guaranteeing the freedom all Americans—including students—have to practice the religion they identify with.

Other Americans, however, argue that Christian values are inseparable from other democratic principles and contribute to the education of U.S. students in and out of the classroom. They claim that the authors of the U.S. Constitution never intended to separate church and state and cite founders such as John Jay, the first chief justice of the United States, who said, "It is the duty of all wise, free and virtuous governments to countenance and encourage virtue and religion."[36] When it comes to public education, proponents of both sides of this issue have battled throughout history for the authority to determine how children are taught and what rights they have to practice their own religion in school.

Some people believe politicians should make laws according to Christian values. These people tend to believe the Founding Fathers would have done the same themselves. However, it is impossible to know exactly what the Founding Fathers, such as George Washington, Thomas Jefferson, and John Adams, would think of religion in the United States today.

Interpreting the Separation of Church and State

The principal legal precedent regulating the relationship between the church and the state comes from a section of the First Amendment to the U.S. Constitution. It states, "Congress shall make no law respecting an establishment of religion, or prohibiting the free exercise thereof." The first element of this statement is known as the establishment clause and ensures religious freedom for all by protecting citizens from having to follow laws based on a religion they do not practice or from having their religion restricted. In the 1947 Supreme Court case *Everson v.*

Board of Education, the Court defined the establishment clause in this way:

> *Neither a state nor the Federal Government can set up a church. Neither can pass laws which aid one religion, aid all religions, or prefer one religion over another. Neither can force or influence a person to go to or remain away from church against his will or force him to profess a belief or disbelief in any religion ... No tax in any amount, large or small, can be levied to support any religious activities or institutions, whatever they may be called, or whatever form they may adopt to teach or practice religion. Neither a state nor the Federal Government can, openly or secretly, participate in the affairs of any religious organizations or groups and vice versa.*[37]

To deal with the establishment issue, the Supreme Court created a three-part test to determine the proper boundary between church and state. The test asks whether or not a government action fulfills a clear secular (nonreligious) purpose, whether or not it either promotes or suppresses religion as its main effect, and whether or not it avoids unnecessary entanglement with religion. These three conditions are generally at the heart of the Supreme Court's judgment in cases related to the association of government with religion.

The second element of the First Amendment section on religion, known as the free exercise clause, protects individuals from being prevented by the government from practicing their religion. For students, this clause gives them the right to believe whatever religious doctrine they desire. Furthermore, the government—including public schools paid for with government money—cannot force students' belief, punish their expression of religious belief, or lend its power to any side in a religious controversy. This is why religious schools—which generally follow Christianity—are private schools that do not receive government funding and therefore do not have to give their students the same rights public school students are guaranteed. In a religious private school, students can be required to do things such as pray every day and attend religious education classes no matter what religion they practice at home.

Praying in School

The issue of prayer in public schools is complex. People disagree on nearly all aspects of it: Should schools require students to pray? Should students be allowed to show their religious affiliation—for example, by wearing a cross necklace—and should they be allowed to pray either publicly or privately in school?

Some people believe that if public schools offered optional or mandatory Bible study classes, problems such as bullying would decrease. Others believe secular measures, such as social awareness campaigns, would be more effective in addressing such issues.

Some Americans support a movement to "put God back in schools," believing it will create a sense of unity and morality they feel has been lacking recently. However, people with this view sometimes disagree on how this could best be done. Some people support optional classes, such as Bible study, that students can choose to take. Others believe schools should lead students in mandatory Christian prayer. People who hold this view tend to argue that when schools do not include religious materials, they automatically prioritize atheism, or the lack of belief in a god, over religion. Since separation of church and state protects atheists as well, some religious people believe this is unfair treatment.

Other Americans believe in forbidding any obvious religious expression in public places, including public schools. Proponents of a clear separation between church and state believe that when school officials lead or encourage prayer among students, they clearly violate the establishment clause. Furthermore, they note that most people who support religious expression in schools are speaking only of Christianity. People of other faiths, especially Islam, are often targeted if they practice their religion in school. Opponents of religion in schools tend to see any type of religious class or club as a threat to the separation of church and state.

THE PROBLEM WITH MANDATORY CHRISTIANITY IN SCHOOLS

"Anything that might send a message to our children that you have to be a Christian to be a full American is extremely problematic."

– Amanda Tyler, executive director of the Baptist Joint Committee for Religious Liberty

Quoted in Crystal Woodall, "Trump Celebrates Efforts to Put God and Bible Back in Schools," CBN News, January 28, 2019, www1.cbn.com/cbnnews/politics/2019/january/trump-celebrates-efforts-to-put-god-and-bible-back-in-schools.

The constitutionality of religious practices in schools has generally been determined in the courts. A landmark case that illustrates the competing principles in the free exercise and establishment clauses is *Engel v. Vitale*, brought by the parents of 10 students in New York in 1962. The students' school district required each student to recite this prayer at the beginning of each school day: "Almighty God, we acknowledge our dependence upon Thee, and we beg Thy blessings upon us, our parents, our teachers, and our Country."[38] The parents argued that the prayer went against the beliefs of their children and that any religious expression in public school violated the establishment clause of the First Amendment. The school board countered that the prayer was nondenominational and could appeal to all religious views. Moreover, they said, students who did not want to recite the prayer were allowed to remain silent. To eliminate the prayer would be to take away other students' free exercise of religion.

The Supreme Court sided with the parents. Justice Hugo L. Black wrote the majority opinion for the Court, saying that "a union of government and religion tends to destroy government and to degrade religion."[39] The case set a clear precedent that declared organized school prayer to be unconstitutional. According to the precedent, schools must not give the impression that they endorse religious belief over nonbelief or any one particular belief over others.

This court case has led to some confusion about what is allowed and what is not in school. Some people interpreted the Court's decision to mean that no religion whatsoever was allowed in schools. In reality, as long as they do so outside of instructional time, students are generally permitted to lead other, like-minded students in religious activities or practice their faith alone because their freedom to practice their religion is protected. This means that a student who says a quiet prayer before eating lunch, a group of students who want to start a Bible study club, and a student who says "Merry Christmas" to their classmates are all protected. Schools cannot forbid students from practicing their freedom of religion unless it meets two broad criteria: "it (a) materially and substantially interferes with the operation of the school, or (b) infringes on the rights of other students."[40] Student-led religious clubs can meet on school grounds, and they can receive their share of school funding just like any other club.

What Is Allowed?

While prayer led by school officials is clearly banned by the Supreme Court, some students have argued that they should be able to participate in religious activities if they voluntarily seek to do so during extracurricular activities. In some instances, for example, students have asked to open an athletic event by reciting a prayer. Others have volunteered to read a prayer during their graduation ceremonies. They argue that since the prayer is voluntarily offered outside of the classroom, they are not imposing religion on others.

RELIGIOUS EXPRESSION IS PROTECTED

"It's true that some public school officials still misunderstand (or ignore) the First Amendment by censoring student religious expression that is protected under current law. But when challenged in court, they invariably lose."

— Charles C. Haynes, vice president of the Newseum Institute and founding director of the Religious Freedom Center

Quoted in Valerie Strauss, "Can Students Pray in Public Schools? Can Teachers Say 'Merry Christmas'? What's Allowed—and What's Forbidden," *Washington Post*, December 24, 2016, www.washingtonpost.com/news/answer-sheet/wp/2016/12/24/can-students-pray-in-public-schools-can-teachers-say-merry-christmas-whats-allowed-and-forbidden/?utm_term=.313c1590164f.

Opponents have objected to prayer in these settings as well as in more formal educational situations. The problem cited in such cases is that student-led prayer constitutes peer pressure around religious practices. Legal suits contesting prayer during extracurricular activities have reached the Supreme Court, where decisions have consistently ruled that prayer is unconstitutional. For example, in the 2000 case of *Santa Fe Independent School District v. Doe*, the Court ruled that a student who led a pre-game prayer at several high school football games did violate the establishment clause because not everyone present wanted to participate in the prayer. However, in line with the free exercise clause of the First Amendment, students have been allowed to engage in voluntary individual prayer, as long as it does not disrupt the educational mission of the school. Charles C. Haynes, vice president of the Newseum Institute and founding director of the Religious Freedom Center, explained:

Truth be told, students of all faiths are actually free to pray alone or in groups during the school day, as long as they don't disrupt

the school or interfere with the rights of others. Of course, the right to engage in voluntary prayer or religious discussion does not necessarily include the right to preach to a captive audience, like an assembly, or to compel other students to participate.[41]

According to U.S. law as of 2019, public school staff are not allowed to require students to pray with them. However, the student-athletes on this Catholic school football team could be required to pray no matter what religion they follow.

Other controversial forms of student religious practices include off-campus activities during school time and religious clubs. The legality of off-campus events came into question in 1952 when students in New York were released during the school day to participate in activities at religious centers away from school grounds. Students whose families chose not to participate in the release program stayed at school. When some objected to the religious activity during school hours, the

Supreme Court heard the case. By a 6–3 vote, the Court ruled that off-campus release time programs that are not mandatory for all students are permissible accommodations of the religious needs of students and do not violate the establishment clause of the Constitution.

More recently, controversy has arisen over the rights of students to pray on campus. Several news articles have incorrectly stated that in some states, Muslim students are allowed to pray on campus but Christian students are not, stirring up anti-Muslim sentiment and leading to calls to ban Muslim students from praying during school hours. In 2017, National Public Radio (NPR) reported on a Texas school that opened an

Unlike Christian prayers, Muslim prayers must be performed a certain way—for example, the people who are praying must remove their shoes and face a specific direction—so allowing Muslim students to use a free classroom gives them the same freedom to exercise their religion that their non-Muslim classmates have.

on-campus prayer room, creating much debate. Some people thought no prayer at all should be allowed on campus and that a prayer room meant the school was endorsing religious activity. Others disagreed, noting that it was not mandatory for students to pray there. The room was originally opened because some Muslim students were leaving campus on Fridays to go to a nearby mosque to pray, causing them to miss up to two hours of the school day. In an effort to balance their students' religious freedom and educational needs, the school opened the prayer room but also made it available to students of all faiths who wanted to use it. This is considered a release time program similar to the one that was the focus of the 1952 case.

American Opposition to French Law

In 2004, France passed a law to prohibit the wearing of noticeable religious clothing in public schools as a matter of maintaining a strict separation of church and state. The law included a ban on Muslim girls wearing hijabs in school, and many people around the world viewed it as a deliberate attack on the religious freedom of Muslims, since no other religion has been targeted so aggressively. The U.S. Helsinki Commission, a federal agency made up of members of the House of Representatives and the U.S. Departments of State, Defense, and Commerce, filed a statement in reaction to the French law. The purpose of the Helsinki Commission is to monitor compliance with the Helsinki Accords of 1975, an international agreement among several countries—including the United States and France—to enforce certain human rights, including the rights to freedom of religion and freedom of speech. Helsinki Commission chairman Christopher H. Smith firmly denounced the law, saying, "I urge French authorities to rethink their policy and make reasonable accommodations for students to wear religious dress. Expelling children is not the answer. Students attending public schools should not have to sacrifice their religious beliefs to enjoy the same educational opportunities as their fellow classmates."[1] According to the Helsinki Commission, the right to wear a hijab should not only be a right for U.S. students, it should be an international right. However, as of 2019, the ban remains in place, and France has placed further restrictions on Islamic dress.

1. Quoted in "Helsinki Commission Leaders Alarmed at French Students' Expulsion over Religious Attire," International Information Programs, November 4, 2004. usinfo.state.gov/dhr/Archive/2004/Nov/05-862094.html.

Religious Symbols

Another controversy over religious freedom concerns religious symbols and clothing in school. Legal decisions in the United States have generally supported the right of schools to adopt dress codes to regulate student appearance; however, the courts have not allowed schools to ban any particular religious attire, such as cross necklaces or hijabs.

Bahai	Buddhist	Buddhist
Christian	Christian	Confucian
	Hindu	Confucian/Taoist
Islamic	Sikh	Shinto

In public schools, teachers are only allowed to use religious symbols such as these as teaching aids, not decoration.

Furthermore, teachers are not allowed to display religious symbols in the classroom as a form of decoration, as this has been considered a promotion of the religion associated with the symbol. This means, for example, a teacher in a public school cannot have a Christian crucifix or Jewish Star of David permanently on display in their classroom.

However, exceptions for religious symbols are made in specific circumstances, such as when the teacher is using the symbol to illustrate a concept in class. For instance, starting in September 1941, the Nazis required Jewish people in Germany and German-occupied countries to wear yellow badges shaped like the Star of David to identify themselves. Students learning about the Holocaust in a history class may be shown the Star of David; this is not considered a violation of the restrictions on the use of religious symbols. The courts have ruled that "teachers can teach about religion as long as (a) the content is tied to academic objectives and (b) teachers do not attempt to indoctrinate students to a certain religious belief or nonbelief."[42]

Furthermore, certain symbols have gained secular popularity, so the courts have ruled that those particular symbols are allowed. Around the holidays, Christmas trees and menorahs can be displayed in schools as decorations as long as there is no ceremony accompanying them; for example, the school cannot require students to gather together to light the menorah each day or place a Nativity scene under the Christmas tree. Generally, if one secularized religious symbol is permitted, others must be as well. For instance, if a school puts up a Christmas tree, it is not allowed to ban the menorah.

School Vouchers

Another controversy in education today is the issue of school choice. School choice debates stem from the fact that several different school systems exist in the United States, yet only public schools are supported by tax dollars. Parents who prefer to send their children to private schools have argued that they are at an economic disadvantage. Since the private schools receive no state support, parents have to pay tuition to the schools in order for children to attend. Some parents argue that this additional economic burden is particularly unfair when they want their children to attend religious school. Since no religious education is available in free public schools, they believe they essentially have to pay for their religious freedom, creating an unconstitutional burden. Others disagree, noting that religion is not forbidden in public schools and that there are extracurricular religious education programs available that are much cheaper than a private school education.

Private school classes tend to be smaller, which means students can receive more attention from their teachers if they are struggling with classwork. This is one of the reasons why many people want to send their children to private schools.

Proponents of broader school choice argue that students should be able to attend private schools whether or not they can afford the tuition. In addition to the issue of religion, there is a widespread belief that the quality of education is better at private schools, although the truth of this depends greatly on the schools and the areas of the country where they are located. Nobel Prize–winning economist Milton Friedman proposed a plan to give low-income parents vouchers to lessen the cost of tuition if they want to send their children to private and religious schools. In his plan, the government would pay most of the private school tuition to ensure that all students could choose the type of school they preferred. Defenders of voucher programs say that such government assistance does not violate the establishment clause because government assistance is already available for some secular services in religious schools. For example, Pennsylvania and New Jersey allocate funding for textbooks, testing, and other services for private school students. In June 1998, the Supreme Court of Wisconsin ruled in favor of the Milwaukee Parental Choice Program, which provides financial assistance to low-income children who want to attend private and religious schools.

Opponents of school voucher programs object to government assistance on several grounds. They assert that state funding has a primary effect of advancing religion if it is channeled to religious schools. Such an entanglement would violate the establishment clause by blurring the division between church and state. Furthermore, if tax dollars are funneled to private schools, they fear that public schools will suffer from budget cuts as limited funding is spread to more institutions. The U.S. Supreme Court settled the constitutionality of the issue in the 2002 case *Zelman v. Simmons-Harris*. According to the website EdChoice, "The justices made it very clear that when an individual uses public funds to make a private choice—in this case when a parent uses a voucher to send his or her child to a private school (including religious schools)—it does not violate the First Amendment."[43] However, some people continue to oppose the program for religious and other reasons.

Evolution versus Creationism

Debates over what should and should not be taught in public schools have sometimes centered on religious content. These debates most often pit science-based theories of the creation of the Earth and the universe against religious beliefs. In 1925, one of the most famous court cases in American history marked the educational dilemma caused by the growing popularity of Charles Darwin's theory of evolution. By that time, evolution was achieving scientific authority over the previously preferred creationist theory, which was based on Biblical teachings. A biology teacher in a rural Tennessee town, John T. Scopes, challenged the law that prohibited him from teaching about evolution. His lawyer, Clarence Darrow, argued and eventually won the teacher's case in *State of Tennessee v. Scopes*—also known as the "Scopes Monkey Trial" because Darwin's theory linked humans to other primates. However, the decision came out of the state supreme court and therefore affected only the law in Tennessee.

The creation of the universe, including the formation of the natural world and the development of human life, has been explained in various ways by different religious groups as well as by scientists such as Charles Darwin.

Forty years later, another teacher had to challenge a similar law in Arkansas. In 1965, Susan Epperson, a biology teacher in Little Rock, Arkansas, argued that she should be able to teach the theory of evolution. In a unanimous decision, the Supreme Court held that states are not allowed to forbid teachers from teaching things that go against any religious beliefs. The decision declared that any ban on teaching the theory of evolution violates the establishment clause.

Struggles over teaching creationism versus evolution continue in spite of the decision. Advocates of teaching creationism passed laws in Arkansas and Louisiana requiring the teaching of "creation science" in all public school courses that taught evolutionary theory. In 1987, a group of parents, teachers, and religious leaders challenged the Louisiana law, taking their case all the way to the U.S. Supreme Court in *Edwards v. Aguillard*. In a 7–2 decision, the Court held that the law was intended to promote religion and therefore violated the establishment clause. Although this was a clear-cut decision that would seem to have settled the issue, similar laws have been proposed—but not passed—since then. For example, in 2019, Indiana proposed a law that would allow schools "to teach 'creation science' as an alternative to the scientific theory of evolution … [and] requires public schools to display a poster stating 'In God We Trust' in each classroom and library."[44] Oklahoma proposed similar laws in 2017 and 2019. Various secular groups, such as the Center for Inquiry, have promised to fight the passage of these bills.

It is important to remember that the Supreme Court has made clear that instruction about religion in public schools is constitutional. However, decisions on court cases have required that religion must be taught objectively and neutrally. According to legal precedent, the purpose of public schools is to educate students about a variety of religious traditions, not to promote one religion or indoctrinate students into any specific faith tradition.

CHAPTER 5

Privacy Rights

Privacy is one of the most hotly debated topics between teens and adults. Some adults believe people under the age of 18 have no right to privacy, either at home or at school. Many young adults believe this to be untrue. While the courts generally do not get involved in the rules parents set for their own children, they have set some guidelines for what kind of privacy students can expect in public schools. However, like other student rights issues, a student's right to privacy is frequently debated. Students may feel that their schools are not lenient enough, while some parents and teachers believe schools should be stricter. In many cases, students and adults alike are unaware of what privacy rights students actually have.

The issue of privacy in schools pits students' personal rights against the schools' obligation to keep students safe from harm—from each other, from outsiders, and from themselves. When does an individual's privacy compromise the safety or educational experience of another student or teacher? In recent years, this issue has been especially contentious in relation to the search and seizure of students and their property, and in regard to policies about testing students for drug use and keeping them safe from school shooters.

Search and Seizure

In the United States, the legal limits of a person's right to privacy are defined in the Fourth Amendment to the U.S. Constitution.

The Fourth Amendment ensures "the right of the people to be secure in their persons, houses, papers, and effects, against unreasonable searches and seizures." Police officers and government agents cannot search a home or a person who is going about their normal business without a search warrant issued by a judge and based on probable cause that a crime has been committed.

However, schools function more like workplaces in regard to privacy. Government workplaces, such as courtrooms and libraries, are similar to public schools in that the laws of the Constitution apply to the employers. Private workplaces, however—anything owned by an individual or non-governmental company, such as a bank or store—function more like private schools, where employers have more freedom to make rules that limit their employees' privacy. A person who accepts a job at such an institution, just like a student who attends a private school, agrees to abide by these rules.

In a public school or government workplace, citizens have the expectation of a certain amount of privacy. School officials cannot randomly search a student's purse, car, or other possessions without a good reason, such as a valid suspicion that the student has brought drugs or weapons to school. Reasonable searches are allowed when the safety or health of the staff and students might be in danger. Due to the recent attention on school violence, many schools have installed metal detectors at their entrances that can locate concealed weapons. In some school districts, all students are subject to body searches before entering school buildings. After the Parkland shooting, the administration of Marjory Stoneman Douglas High School required all students to carry clear backpacks so any weapons would be visible. The students complied with the new policy but mocked the backpacks through memes and political statements. Twitter and Instagram accounts featured pictures of some of the most creatively decorated backpacks. Many stated that they did not believe the backpacks made them safer; some demonstrated their point by simply positioning a folder or sheet of paper in the backpack in such a way that it blocked all the other contents from sight.

Marjory Stoneman Douglas students did not attempt to bring a case to court regarding the school's new clear backpack policy. Instead, they mocked the backpacks on the internet, accusing school officials of not thinking carefully enough about the ways dangerous items could still be hidden from sight in the backpacks.

More and more schools have also started to perform random searches of student lockers and desks. Such measures are often part of zero-tolerance policies that immediately suspend or expel students carrying weapons or drugs. Some students, parents, and teachers praise strict measures to ensure school safety. Others consider them overly harsh and express concern that the privacy rights of students are being compromised. Some have noted that such strict rules sometimes result in students being punished in ways that may be regarded as unfair. For instance, if a child brings a plastic weapon to school and their belongings are searched, they may be punished even though the toy is harmless and the student may have had no intention of ever taking it out of their bag until they left school grounds.

The courts have provided guidance to school officials on the issue of student searches. A landmark Supreme Court case, *New Jersey v. T.L.O.*, helped define the legal justifications as well as the legal scope for a student search. The case involved a 14-year-old student who was discovered smoking, in violation of school rules. When the student denied smoking, the principal seized and searched her purse. The principal found not only a pack of cigarettes but also rolling papers and other items associated with drug use, a large amount of cash, and notes linking the student to drug deals. When the school brought delinquency charges against the student, her lawyers moved to suppress the evidence found in her purse, claiming that the principal violated her Fourth Amendment rights. The Court ruled in favor of the search and found that the initiation of the search of a student or their belongings requires reasonable grounds for suspecting the search will turn up evidence that the student is violating the law or school rules. This requires some type of evidence; searches based on a student's race, clothing, or other superficial factors are not considered reasonable. Furthermore, the scope of the search must be reasonable based upon the facts surrounding the search. As the ACLU explained,

> School officials may not search you unless they have a good reason to believe that you in particular—not just "someone"—broke a law or a school rule. So, if a teacher thinks she saw you selling drugs to another student, she can ask you to empty your pockets and can search your backpack. But just because they think some students have drugs doesn't give them the authority to search all students.[45]

While the Supreme Court held that students have a legitimate expectation of privacy, a more flexible standard of "reasonableness" for searches of students is necessary to ensure school safety and discipline.

Percentage Distribution of School Discipline by Race (2015–2016)

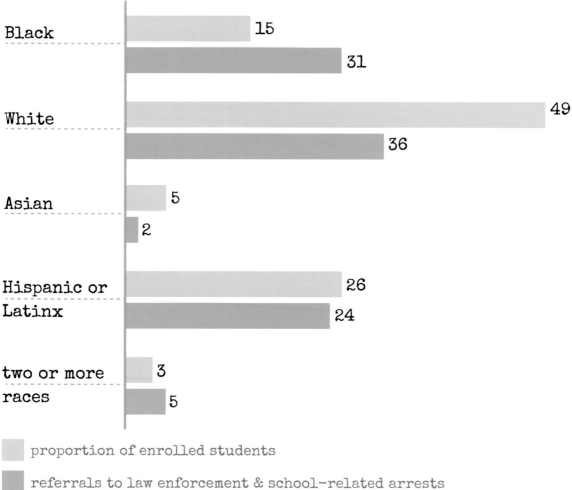

Racial profiling that leads to disciplinary action is a problem in public schools, as this information from the U.S. Department of Education's Office for Civil Rights shows.

LEGAL WITHIN CERTAIN BOUNDARIES

"Given the need for school safety, the authority to conduct searches and reprimand students frequently pre-empts [overrides] a student's right to privacy ... But it's hardly an open invitation. Schools routinely lose court cases when searches they conduct are not reasonable at the start or become too sweeping once they begin."

– Center for Public Education

Search and Seizure Due Process and Public Schools," Center for Public Education, accessed on March 26, 2012, www.centerforpubliceducation.org/research/search-and-seizure-due-process-and-public-schools

The requirement of reasonable suspicion in *New Jersey v. T.L.O.* may seem to rule out broadly used devices and practices such as metal detectors, entrance searches, and random locker or desk searches. However, the courts also recognize the schools' right to set limits on students' expectations of privacy on school grounds or in school property. In general, the courts have allowed schools to conduct suspicionless searches when steps are taken to reduce the reasonable expectation of privacy. For example, a school may send home a letter explaining its policy of random unannounced locker searches at the beginning of each academic year. The notice would serve the function of legally informing students that they should consider lockers to be "public" and not "private" areas. Drug-sniffing dogs and pat-down searches (in which a student is patted down over the clothes by an investigator) have generally been upheld by the courts. Strip searches, on the other hand—where an investigator forces the student to take off items of clothing to prove nothing is hidden underneath them—are considered an invasion of the student's privacy, and some states have laws against them. The legality of locker searches varies by state; some states have ruled that lockers are school property and therefore do not count as a student's personal possession, while other states have ruled that a school official needs a reason to search a student's locker.

Can Teachers Take Students' Phones Away?

Most students today have a cell phone and bring it to school, prompting schools to make rules about the times and places students can use their devices. In some schools, students must keep their phones in their backpack or locker at all times; others may allow students to use their phone if they have a free period. Many schools confiscate the student's phone as a penalty for breaking these rules and give it back after class or after school.

Students frequently object to having their personal property taken, but this is not considered a violation of their rights—as long as the phone is eventually returned to them—because it is a known penalty for their choice to break a school rule. However, it is a violation of their right to privacy if school officials access the information on the phone. According to the Rhode Island branch of the ACLU,

> If they take your phone for a particular reason—for example, another student claims you sent them an inappropriate text message during the school day—they may be allowed to check for that particular message, but they should not be checking additional information on the phone, such as your contact list, photos, etc. If a school official asks for permission to search your phone, you do not have to give your permission.[1]

If a student gets in trouble for something a school official finds on their phone after confiscating it or for denying the school permission to search their phone, or if the school searches the phone even after being denied permission, the student may be able to take their case to court.

1. "Know Your Rights: Students and Technology," American Civil Liberties Union of Rhode Island, August 2017, riaclu.org/documents/RIACLU_pamphlet_StudentRightsTechnology.pdf

Drug Testing in Schools

Mandatory drug testing of students has become a very controversial issue related to students' right to privacy. Since the 1990s, a growing number of schools are requiring drug tests, especially for students who participate in athletics and extracurricular activities. Some schools also perform drug tests at random on the entire student population. Drug abuse, especially the harmful effects of steroid use among young athletes who seek to increase their physical strength, has motivated many schools' testing policies. Supporters of drug testing claim that it can help curb drug addiction in adults as well as youth: Evidence supports the fact that teens who take drugs are at a higher risk of developing a substance use disorder later in life. According to John Walters, former director of the Office of National Drug Control Policy, "[Testing] is a powerful tool at a critical time in young people's lives."[46]

In reaction to the growing trend of requiring drug tests in educational environments, individuals and organizations are raising objections to imposed drug testing. Those against the practice often cite research that finds drug testing to be an ineffective method of discouraging drug use. They point to studies that conclude that the best way to reduce student drug abuse is to encourage stronger social ties and participation in organized activities. Organizations such as the Rutherford Institute, the American Academy of Pediatrics, and the ACLU have argued that requiring drug tests for athletics and clubs deters students from extracurricular activities—an effect that would likely increase drug use rather than decrease it. Furthermore, opponents find drug testing to be overly invasive and often inaccurate. Being subjected to a mandatory test can undercut any sense of

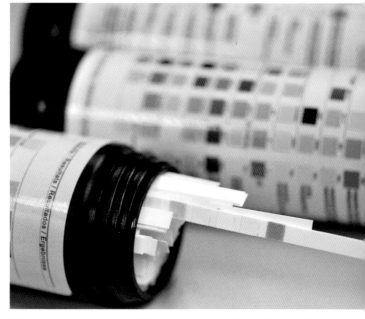

The most common type of drug test is a urinalysis. This kind of testing is also used by doctors to check a person's urine for signs of disease or other health problems.

trust a student has in teachers and administrators. Moreover, a certain small percentage of drug tests, including urinalysis, yield false positive results, and human error can add to inaccuracies. Opponents argue that a student's record could be permanently stained even if a bad test result is ultimately cleared.

First and foremost, though, opponents argue that drug tests undermine students' right to privacy. The Washington Supreme Court heard a privacy case in 2008. The Wankiakum School District had a policy that its schools could test any student for drugs, even if the student was not suspected of using illegal drugs. The ACLU, which represented two families of students in the Wankiakum School District, took the school district to court over the issue. The ACLU said the drug tests violated the students' right to privacy. The Washington Supreme Court ruled that officials should not violate individual privacy when there is no reason to believe that a student has used illegal drugs. Additionally, when a school in Lockney, Texas, became the first institution to require drug testing of all students in grades six through twelve, a federal court struck down the policy as unconstitutional.

RIGHTS WHILE BEING QUESTIONED

"You have the right to remain silent if you're questioned by a school official. Usually there is no problem with answering a few questions to clear something up. But if you think that teacher suspects you of having committed a crime, don't explain, don't lie and don't confess, because anything you say could be used against you. Ask to see your parents or a lawyer."

—ACLU

"Students: Your Right to Privacy," ACLU, accessed on March 26, 2019, www.aclu.org/other/students-your-right-privacy.

The courts' decisions have been different, though, when it comes to drug testing in extracurricular activities. Unlike general school attendance, participation in clubs and sports teams is considered a privilege, not a right. In the 1995 case *Vernonia v. Acton*, the U.S. Supreme Court upheld widespread drug testing of school athletes. According to the decision, student drug testing is allowed only in cases where an individual student is suspected of drug use or where a group of students have shown a high level of use. The Court ruled, however, that this does not apply to school athletes; they have lower expectations of privacy because they are already required to have physical examinations in order to play on a team. The Court also said that testing was justified because athletes engage in dangerous activity in sports. Under the influence of drugs, they would be more likely to injure themselves, and the necessary safety of student athletes is more important than the preservation of their right to privacy. Similarly, in the 2002 case *Board of Education v. Earls*, the Court upheld random testing of students who participate in nonathletic extracurricular activities, arguing that the tests were a reasonable means of preventing and detecting drug use.

FERPA and Student Records

Another privacy rights issue relates to the way schools keep records of academic and personal progress from kindergarten through college graduation. Schools typically record extensive, and sometimes highly personal, information about students and their families for educational purposes. Collecting and storing this information has the potential to intrude on student privacy, but in most cases, it helps teachers, counselors, and other professionals provide the best instruction and guidance for students. The question is how to maintain a reasonable balance between the individual's right to privacy and the school's need to know information related to its educational mission.

This issue came into the public eye in the late 1960s and 1970s, when a rising number of people—especially young people—insisted on their First Amendment right to freedom of speech and engaged in protests against societal discrimination and government policies. Demonstrating their support of civil rights, women's liberation, and the anti-Vietnam War movement, they came under the suspicion of law enforcement. Americans gained a new awareness about the extent to which various government institutions keep written files on the lives and activities of individual citizens. This growing awareness of government record keeping made some people question whether their constitutional right to privacy was being compromised.

Concerned about government record keeping, parents and students sought to have more control over educational information and its distribution. They lobbied for the right to inspect their own educational files in order to know what information was being recorded. They also wanted to prevent schools from giving out personal information unless it was authorized

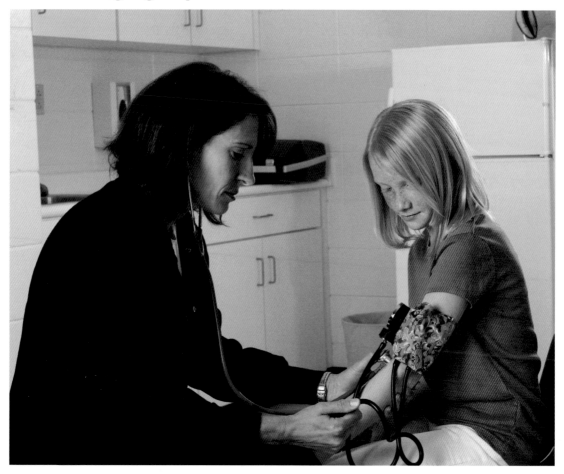

In addition to students' grades and disciplinary records, schools are legally prohibited from releasing the health records kept by the school nurse.

and necessary to a student's educational progress. Their efforts developed into the Family Education Rights and Privacy Act (FERPA), also known as the Buckley Amendment. FERPA took effect on November 19, 1974.

FERPA clearly defines students' right to privacy in school records, files, documents, and other materials. It applies to elementary, secondary, and postsecondary educational agencies that receive federal support, and therefore encompasses all public schools and any private schools that accept federal funding. The U.S. Department of Health and Human Services enforces the act and handles any complaints that arise. FERPA addresses academic records and health information maintained by schools.

Privacy of Grades

Sometimes teachers have students exchange and grade each other's work in class. While most students and parents do not mind this, others are concerned about anyone except the teacher knowing their grades. Kristja Falvo, a mother of three students in Oklahoma schools, told the teachers that the practice embarrassed her children, one of whom threatened to quit school because other students teased him about his test scores. When the teachers and the school refused to stop the peer-grading activities, Falvo sued the school district.

Testifying in defense of the policy, LeRoy Rooker of the U.S. Department of Education argued that peer grading does not violate FERPA because the grades do not become official educational records until after they are recorded in the teacher's gradebook. Teachers also testified that peer grading is a valuable class activity because students do learn from grading each other's work. The case went all the way to the Supreme Court, which issued a final ruling in 2002: Student graders do not act for educational institutions—students only briefly handle material assigned by another, official representative—and are not covered, therefore, by FERPA. Peer grading remains an acceptable practice.

Under FERPA, parents and legally independent students have control over the distribution of all information except basic "directory" information, such as a student's name, address, phone number, and date of birth. Parents and eligible students have the right to inspect and review educational records. If they disagree with the information included in the files, they can request that the school correct the record or allow them to place a statement with the record explaining their objections. Furthermore, schools must get written permission from the parent or eligible student to release information from a student's record except in cases of health and safety emergencies. Finally, schools must notify parents and eligible students of their rights under FERPA annually.

LGBT+ Rights

A religious private school may be able to make rules forbidding students from exhibiting anything other than heterosexual behavior, but in a public school, a student's sexuality is a private matter. Each student can choose whether to be open with their sexuality or to keep it to themselves. The ACLU explained, "Public schools are not allowed to threaten to 'out' students to their families, overlook bullying, force students to wear clothing inconsistent with their gender identity or bar LGBT-themed clubs or attire."[47] However, while the law gives students the right to discuss being gay, the limits about freedom of expression still apply. A student who disrupts their peers' learning environment—for example, by talking out of turn in class or passing notes with a friend—can be punished, even if the subject of their speech is their sexuality. The ACLU notes that speech is not considered a disruption simply because someone else disagrees with it, so if one student complains about another student discussing their sexuality between classes or at lunch, censoring that student is considered a violation of their rights.

The rights of students are clear and virtually unchallenged in some areas but remain controversial in others. Most young adults are never advised of their rights, and many school officials remain unaware as well, which can present a challenge to young adults trying to assert their rights. As the ACLU noted, "A lot of the time, school officials either don't know what the law requires them to do or they're just betting that you won't question what they say. Don't take their word for it!"[48] Students with a good knowledge of their basic rights can become advocates for themselves and their peers, which gives them a way to potentially protect themselves from future violations and also gives them recourse if a violation does occur.

NOTES

Introduction: The Evolution of Education

1. "11 Facts About the History of Education in America," *American Board Blog*, July 1, 2015. www.americanboard.org/blog/11-facts-about-the-history-of-education-in-america/.

Chapter 1: The Right to a Free and Equal Education

2. Quoted in Kenneth Jost, "School Desegregation," *CQ Researcher*, vol. 14, no. 15, April 23, 2004, p. 362. edge.sagepub.com/system/files/Chambliss2e_12.2CQR.pdf.

3. *Brown v. Board of Education of Topeka,* 349 U.S. 483 (1954).

4. Lauren Camera, "The New Segregation," *U.S. News & World Report*, July 26, 2016. www.usnews.com/news/articles/2016-07-26/racial-tensions-flare-as-schools-resegregate.

5. Quoted in Janie Boschma and Ronald Brownstein, "The Concentration of Poverty in American Schools," *The Atlantic*, February 29, 2016. www.theatlantic.com/education/archive/2016/02/concentration-poverty-american-schools/471414/.

6. Quoted in Jenny Jarvie, "School Seeks to End Racial Integration," *Boston Globe*, October 29, 2006. www.boston.com/news/education/k_12/articles/2006/10/29/school_seeks _to_end_racial_integration.

7. Roger Shuler, "School Segregation Is Taking New Forms," *Daily Kos*, January 29, 2010. www.dailykos.com/story/2010/1/29/831859/-.

8. Quoted in David Masci, "Hispanic Americans' New Clout," *CQ Researcher,* vol. 8, no. 35, September 18, 1998. library.cqpress.com/cqresearcher/document.php?id=cqresrre1998091800.

9. Rafi Letzter, "A Physicist Said Women's Brains Make Them Worse at Physics—Experts Say That's 'Laughable,'" Live Science, October 2, 2018. www.livescience.com/63730-physicist-says-women-bad-at-physics.html.

10. Quoted in National Coalition for Women and Girls in Education, "Math and Science Get C+ on Report Card on Gender Equity," IDRA, March 2000. www.idra.org/resource-center/math-and-science-get-c-on-report-card-on-gender-equity/.

11. Quoted in Richard L. Worsnop, "Gender Equity in Sports," *CQ Researcher*, vol. 7, no. 15, April 18, 1997. library.cqpress.com/cqresearcher/document.php?id=cqresrre1997041806.

12. Quoted in Alexandra Gekas, "Q&A: Do We Still Need Title IX," *Newsweek*, June 22, 2007. www.newsweek.com/qa-do-we-still-need-title-ix-102153.

13. Brigid Schulte, "Does Title IX Equality for Females Come at Males' Expense?," *Washington Post*, June 27, 2013. www.washingtonpost.com/local/does-title-ix-equality-for-females-come-at-males-expense/2013/06/27/7c8beee0-df55-11e2-b2d4-ea6d8f477a01_story.html?utm_term=.9a01302dcd8e.

14. Amy Packham, "Girls Play Less Sport Than Boys: Here's How You Can Change That," *HuffPost*, January 31, 2018. www.huffingtonpost.co.uk/entry/how-to-encourage-girls-sport_uk_5a704e2ce4b0a52682ff3da0.

15. Quoted in Packham, "Girls Play Less Sport."

Chapter 2: Freedom of Expression

16. Allison Fiddler, "Question of the Week: Should the Pledge of Allegiance Be Required in Schools?," Daily American, October 10, 2018. www.dailyamerican.com/entertainment/highschoolhighlights/question-of-the-week-should-the-pledge-of-allegiance-be/article_c89bddd4-01ae-54de-a43e-89f288701fa0.html.

17. Tessa Lynn, "Question of the Week: Should the Pledge of Allegiance Be Required in Schools?," Daily American, October 10, 2018. www.dailyamerican.com/entertainment/highschoolhighlights/question-of-the-week-should-the-pledge-of-allegiance-be/article_c89bddd4-01ae-54de-a43e-89f288701fa0.html.

18. Kaitlyn Carney, "Question of the Week: Should the Pledge of Allegiance Be Required in Schools?," Daily American, October 10, 2018. www.dailyamerican.com/entertainment/highschoolhighlights/question-of-the-week-should-the-pledge-of-allegiance-be/article_c89bddd4-01ae-54de-a43e-89f288701fa0.html.

19. David L. Hudson Jr. and Freddie Wolf, "Pledge of Allegiance," Freedom Forum Institute, last updated September 18, 2017. www.freedomforuminstitute.org/first-amendment-center/topics/freedom-of-speech-2/k-12-public-school-student-expression/pledge-of-allegiance/.

20. Galen Sherwin, "5 Things Public Schools Can and Can't Do When It Comes to Dress Codes," ACLU, May 30, 2017. www.aclu.org/blog/womens-rights/womens-rights-education/5-things-public-schools-can-and-cant-do-when-it-comes.

21. Sherwin, "5 Things Public Schools Can and Can't Do."

22. Hayley Krischer, "Is Your Body Appropriate to Wear to School?," New York Times, April 17, 2018. www.nytimes.com/2018/04/17/style/student-bra-nipples-school.html.

23. "Students' Rights: Speech, Walkouts, and Other Protests,"

ACLU, accessed on March 7, 2019. www.aclu.org/issues/free-speech/student-speech-and-privacy/students-rights-speech-walkouts-and-other-protests.

24. "Your Rights: Student Social Media Rights," ACLU of Northern California, accessed on March 8, 2019. www.aclunc.org/our-work/know-your-rights/student-social-media-rights.

25. "Your Rights," ACLU of Northern California.

26. David R. Wheeler, "Do Students Still Have Free Speech in School?," *The Atlantic,* April 7, 2014. www.theatlantic.com/education/archive/2014/04/do-students-still-have-free-speech-in-school/360266/.

27. "Student Media Guide to Maintaining an Off-Campus Website," Student Press Law Center, August 25, 2014. splc.org/2014/08/student-media-guide-to-maintaining-an-off-campus-web-site/.

Chapter 3: Freedom of the School Press

28. Quoted in "Jefferson's Preference for 'Newspapers without Government' over 'Government without Newspapers' (1787)," Online Library of Liberty, accessed on April 19, 2019. oll.libertyfund.org/quotes/302.

29. Nicholas D. Kristof, *Freedom of the High School Press.* Lanham, MD: University Press of America, 1983, p. 3.

30. Quoted in Diane Divoky, ed., *How Old Will You Be in 1984?* New York, NY: Discuss, 1969, p. 2.

31. *Draudt v. Wooster City School District Board of Education*, 246 F. Supp. 2d 820 (N.D. Ohio 2003).

32. *Beussink v. Woodland R-IV School District*, 30 F. Supp. 2d 1175 (E.D. Mo. 1998).

33. *Beussink v. Woodland R-IV School District.*

34. Quoted in Moriah Balingit, "A Principal Yanked a Drug Article from a Student Newspaper, so It Ran Online," *Washington Post*, April 5, 2015. www.washingtonpost.com/local/education/a-principal-yanked-a-drug-article-from-a-student-newspaper-so-it-ran-online/2015/04/05/26588068-d4ce-11e4-ab77-9646eea6a4c7_story.html?utm_term=.6ff5e6bcbd75.

35. Quoted in Balingit, "A Principal Yanked a Drug Article from a Student Newspaper."

Chapter 4: Freedom of Religion

36. John Jay, in *The Speeches of the Different Governors to the Legislature of the State of New York, Commencing with those of George Clinton and Continued Down to the Present Time.* Albany, NY: J.B. Van Steenbergh, 1825, p. 66.

37. *Everson v. Board of Education,* 330 U.S. 1 (1947).

38. Quoted in Jamin B. Raskin, *We the Students: Supreme Court Cases for and About Students.* Washington, D.C: CQ Press, 2008, p. 81.

39. *Engel v. Vitale,* 370 U.S. 421 (1962).

40. "Louisiana Just Put God Back in Its Schools: How They Did It," *Christian Patriot Daily*, accessed on March 22, 2019. www.christianpatriotdaily.com/articles/louisiana-just-put-god-back-in-its-schools-how-they-did-it/.

41. Quoted in Valerie Strauss, "Can Students Pray in Public Schools? Can Teachers Say 'Merry Christmas'? What's Allowed—and What's Forbidden," *Washington Post*, December 24, 2016. www.washingtonpost.com/news/answer-sheet/wp/2016/12/24/can-students-pray-in-public-schools-can-teachers-say-merry-christmas-whats-allowed-and-forbidden/?utm_term=.313c1590164f.

42. Quoted in Strauss, "Can Students Pray in Public Schools?"

43. "Are School Choice Programs Legal?," EdChoice, accessed on March 22, 2019. www.edchoice.org/school_choice_faqs/are-school-choice-programs-legal/.

44. "Indiana Anti-Evolution Bill Would Indoctrinate Students in Creationism," Center for Inquiry, January 14, 2019. centerforinquiry.org/press_releases/indiana-anti-evolution-bill-would-indoctrinate-students-in-creationism/.

Chapter 5: Privacy Rights

45. "Students: Your Right to Privacy," ACLU, accessed on March 26, 2019. www.aclu.org/other/students-your-right-privacy.

46. Quoted in Sara B. Miller, "Steps Toward More Drug Testing in Schools," *Christian Science Monitor*, May 20, 2005. www.csmonitor.com/2005/0520/p01s04-ussc.htm.

47. Brian Tashman, "Student Rights at School: Six Things You Need to Know," ACLU, September 1, 2017. www.aclu.org/blog/juvenile-justice/student-rights-school-six-things-you-need-know.

48. "Know Your Rights! A Guide for LGBT High School Students," ACLU, accessed on March 27, 2019. www.aclu.org/sites/default/files/field_document/kyr_at_school_handout_11.24.14_0.pdf.

DISCUSSION QUESTIONS

Chapter 1: The Right to a Free and Equal Education

1. What do you think constitutes a "free and equal" education?

2. Do you think your school is segregated? If so, how do you think this affects you and the other students?

3. Do you think Title IX is still necessary in regard to both education and sports? Why or why not?

Chapter 2: Freedom of Expression

1. Do you think standing for the Pledge of Allegiance should be required? Why or why not?

2. How do you feel about your school's dress code?

3. What policies, if any, do you think schools should be allowed to make regarding internet use on or off campus?

Chapter 3: Freedom of the School Press

1. Do you believe that school newspapers should have the right to print anything they want? If not, what kinds of restrictions would you place on the things they publish?

2. Do you think turning a journalist without a press pass away from a sold-out event can be considered censorship of the press? Why or why not?

3. What is the difference between a "public" and a "nonpublic" forum?

Chapter 4: Freedom of Religion

1. What are some contexts in which a religious symbol could be used as a teaching aid?

2. Do you believe public schools should be allowed to provide a prayer room for students? Why or why not?

3. Should public schools teach creationism?

Chapter 5: Privacy Rights

1. What are some situations that would give a school official a good reason to conduct a search of a student's possessions?

2. Do you agree with the Supreme Court's decision in *Board of Education v. Earls*? Why or why not?

3. Do you think your school does a good job advising you of your rights? If not, how could it improve?

ORGANIZATIONS TO CONTACT

American Civil Liberties Union (ACLU)
125 Broad Street, 18th Floor
New York, NY 10004
www.aclu.org
twitter.com/aclu
www.youtube.com/aclu

> The ACLU is a national organization that defends the rights
> guaranteed in the U.S. Constitution. It works to establish equality
> before the law—regardless of race, color, sexual orientation, or
> national origin—and adamantly opposes regulation of all forms
> of speech, including student journalism and campus hate speech.
> Students can report violations of their rights through the
> "Contact" section of the ACLU's website.

Foundation for Individual Rights in Education (FIRE)
510 Walnut Street, Suite 1250
Philadelphia, PA 19106
www.thefire.org
www.instagram.com/thefireorg
twitter.com/TheFIREorg
www.youtube.com/thefireorg

> The mission of FIRE is to defend individual rights at America's
> colleges and universities, both public and private.

The Freedom Forum Institute
555 Pennsylvania Avenue NW
Washington, DC 20001
www.freedomforum.org
twitter.com/FreedomForumIns

> This organization is dedicated to free press, free speech, and
> other First Amendment rights. It sponsors conferences,
> educational guides, publications, broadcasting, online services,
> and other programs.

Student Press Law Center (SPLC)
1608 Rhode Island Avenue NW, Suite 211
Washington, DC 20036
www.splc.org
www.instagram.com/studentpresslawcenter
twitter.com/SPLC

> The SPLC is a nonprofit organization devoted to educating high
> school and college student journalists about their First
> Amendment rights. The organization provides free legal advice
> to support the student news media and to combat censorship in
> educational environments.

FOR MORE INFORMATION

Books

Braun, Eric. *Never Again: The Parkland Shooting and the Teen Activists Leading a Movement.* Minneapolis, MN: Lerner Publications, 2019.
> This book details the student activist movement surrounding the debate over gun control that has sparked related debates about students' right to protest at school.

Freedman, Russell. *In Defense of Liberty: The Story of America's Bill of Rights.* New York, NY: Scholastic, 2004.
> Freedman discusses the formation and application of the first 10 amendments to the U.S. Constitution.

Klein, Rebecca T. *Your Legal Rights in School.* New York, NY: Rosen Publishing, 2015.
> This book examines the rights students are given by the U.S. legal system.

Mason, Jenny. *Freedom of Speech.* New York, NY: Gareth Stevens Publishing, 2017.
> Historical context and modern court cases give readers a better understanding of their right to free speech.

Rokutani, John. *Freedom of Speech, the Press, and Religion: The First Amendment.* New York, NY: Enslow Publishing, 2018.
> This book examines the First Amendment, the protections it grants, and controversies surrounding it.

Websites

Electronic Frontier Foundation (EFF)
www.eff.org

The EFF works to protect privacy and freedom of expression in the arena of computers and the internet. The organization advocates for student access to computer information and freedom of student speech online.

First Amendment Schools (FAS)
www.firstamendmentschools.org

FAS is a joint project sponsored by the Association for Supervision and Curriculum Development and the First Amendment Center to help schools affirm First Amendment principles through their activities and policies. The organization focuses on preserving five fundamental freedoms for students and teachers: freedom of religion, speech, press, assembly, and petition.

The Freechild Institute
www.freechild.org

The Freechild Institute was created to encourage young people to seek active roles in their schools and communities. The organization promotes social change led by and with young people around the world, particularly those who have been historically denied the right to participate.

Kids, Know Your Rights!
www.ala.org/alsc/sites/ala.org.alsc/files/content/issuesadv/intellectualfreedom/kidsknowyourrights.pdf

This pamphlet, published by the American Library Association's Intellectual Freedom Committee, explains intellectual freedom and the right to privacy.

National Youth Rights Association (NYRA)
www.youthrights.org

NYRA works to educate communities about the rights students have, encourage young adults to get involved in the defense of their own rights, and fight discrimination against young people.

INDEX

A

activism, 9
American Civil Liberties Union (ACLU), 35–36, 39, 41–42, 77, 80–82, 86
Americans with Disabilities Act (ADA), 17

B

baby boom, 9, 32
Beussink v. Woodland R-IV School District (1998), 54
bilingual education, 18–20
Black, Hugo L., 63
Board of Education v. Earls (2002), 83
Boston Latin School, 6–7
Bowern, Claire, 19
boys, 6–7, 20, 22, 24–26, 32–33, 35
Brown v. Board of Education of Topeka (1954), 12

C

Carney, Kaitlyn, 30
cell phones, 39, 80
censorship, 42–46, 48, 50, 53, 56–57
churches, 34, 60
Civil Rights Act of 1964, 12
civil rights movement, 10, 12
creationism, 72–73
cyberbullying, 41

D

desegregation, 12–15
Dewey, John, 8
Draudt v. Wooster City School District Board of Education (2003), 50, 52
dress codes, 32–36
drugs, 56, 75–77, 81–83
drug testing, 80–83

E

Edwards v. Aguillard (1987), 73
Engel v. Vitale (1962), 62
equality, 10, 13, 18, 20–23, 27
Everson v. Board of Education (1947), 59–60
evolution, 72–73
extracurricular activities, 23, 36, 63–64, 81–83

F

Family Education Rights and Privacy Act (FERPA), 85–86
Ferriero, Laura, 18
Fiddler, Allison, 29
First Amendment, 28, 31, 50–52, 58–60, 63–64, 71, 83
Founding Fathers, 59
Fourth Amendment, 74–75, 77
France, 67
freedom of expression, 28, 32, 44, 54, 86
freedom of religion, 34, 58, 63, 67

freedom of speech, 30, 39, 45, 54, 57, 67, 83
freedom of the press, 44, 47, 51

G
girls, 6–7, 20, 22, 24–27, 33–36, 67
Goodman, Mark, 42–43
grades, 17, 84–85
Greenberger, Marcia D., 23–24, 26

H
Haynes, Charles C., 64
Hazelwood School District v. Kuhlmeier (1988), 47–49, 52, 54
Hiestand, Mike, 42–43
hijabs, 34, 67–68
Hudson, David L., Jr., 31

I
immigrants, 13, 18
Individualized Education Program (IEP), 17
Individuals with Disabilities Education Act (IDEA), 17
internet, 9, 39–40, 42–43, 47, 54, 56, 76
Islam, 34, 62, 67

J
Jay, John, 58
Jeck, David, 56
Jefferson, Thomas, 44, 59
Jones Turner, Rita, 15–16
J.S. v. Bethlehem Area School District (2000), 40

K
Karr v. Schmidt (1972), 32
Kerr, T.J., 24

Kristof, Nicholas D., 45

L
LGBT+, 86
LoMonte, Frank, 56
Lynn, Tessa, 30

M
Marshall, Thurgood, 12, 14
Martinez, Lizzy, 33
Massachusetts Bay Colony, 6

N
Negron, Francisco, 37
New Jersey v. T.L.O. (1985), 77, 79
newspapers, 44–52, 54–56

P
Paige, Rod, 11
Parkland shooting, 36, 38, 75
Pledge of Allegiance, 29–30, 32, 41
prayer rooms, 67
praying, 41, 60–67
privacy, 48, 74–75, 77–80, 82–85
private education, 20, 41, 60, 69–71, 75, 85–86
public education, 6, 10, 12–15, 18, 40–41, 58, 60–65, 67–70, 72–75, 78, 85–86

R
records, 82–86
religious symbols, 68–69
Roberto Alvarez v. the Board of Trustees of the Lemon Grove School District (1931), 13

S
Sands, Michael, 31

Santa Fe Independent School District v. Doe (2000), 64
searches, 75–79
segregation, 11–16, 20
Shuler, Roger, 16
Smith, Christopher H., 67
social media, 35, 39, 41–42
sports, 24–27, 82–83

T

State of Tennessee v. Scopes (1925), 72
Tinker v. Des Moines Independent Community School District (1969), 36, 47–48, 52, 54
Title IX, 21–27
Tyler, Amanda, 62

U

U.S. Constitution, 6–7, 58–59, 66, 74–75
U.S. Department of Education, 26, 78, 85

U.S. Supreme Court, 10, 12, 14, 28, 30–31, 47–48, 52, 54, 59–60, 63–66, 71, 73, 77–78, 83, 85

V

Vernonia v. Acton (1995), 83
Vietnam War, 36, 46, 83
vouchers, 71

W

walkouts, 36–38
Walters, John, 81
Warren, Earl, 12
weapons, 75–77
West Virginia Board of Education v. Barnette (1943), 30–32

Z

Zelman v. Simmons-Harris (2002), 71

PICTURE CREDITS

ABOUT THE AUTHOR

Anna Collins lives in Buffalo, NY, with her dog, Fitzgerald, and her husband, Jason, whom she met on a road trip across the United States. She loves coffee and refuses to write without having a full pot ready.